THE COLLEGE G
TO EVERY

Christie Garton

SOURCEBOOKS, INC.
NAPERVILLE, ILLINOIS

Published by Sourcebooks, Inc.
P.O. Box 4410, Naperville, Illinois 60567-4410
(630) 961-3900
Fax: (630) 961-2168
www.sourcebooks.com

Library of Congress Cataloging-in-Publication Data

Garton, Christie.
  U chic : the college girl's guide to everything / Christie Garton.
      p. cm.
  Includes index.
  1. College student orientation—United States. 2. Women college students—United
States—Life skills guides. I. Title.
  LB2343.32.G39 2009
  378.1'9822—dc22
                                    2008050866

Printed and bound in Canada
WC 10 9 8 7 6 5 4 3

PRAISE FOR *U CHIC*

"Get ready to be empowered. This isn't just a manual to college, but to life!"
—Stephanie Elizondo Griest, author of *100 Places Every Woman Should Go*

"Lots of clever strategies on how to have a fabulous time at college, combined with wise advice on how to avoid all-too-common mistakes. A great resource for anyone who wants to be a chic college coed."
—Kim Clark, Senior Writer, *U.S.News & World Report*

"Full of fun, sassy advice on how to make the most of a great time of life, *U Chic* makes me yearn for my college days!"
—Marcy McGinnis, Associate Dean, School of Journalism, Stony Brook University

"From the sisterhood of girlfriends who've been there, *U Chic* answers everything a college girl really wants to know."
—Tracey Wong Briggs, former coordinator of *USA TODAY's* All-USA Academic and Teacher Teams

To the women of UniversityChic.com, the
true inspiration behind this book.

contents

• •

CHAPTER 3—HEAD OF THE CLASS

CHAPTER 4—GETTING INVOLVED

CHAPTER 5—TECH ETIQUETTE FOR A FACEBOOK AGE

CHAPTER 6—LOVE LIFE

CHAPTER 7—SORORITY CHIC

CHAPTER 8—HEALTHY AND HAPPY

CHAPTER 9—SURVIVING TEMPTATION ISLAND

foreword

· ·

From Christie Garton, founder and publisher, UniversityChic.com

Without an older sister growing up, I occasionally had to learn things the hard way. There are advantages to not having to stand in anyone's shadow, but there were many times when a little tried-and-true advice could have helped, especially during my first few years in college. I definitely would have not registered for 18 credit hours my first semester in school! After a few detours, roundabouts, and restarts, I eventually found my way through college and into the real world, but things would have been a whole lot easier with the right advice.

This was the inspiration behind the book and UniversityChic. com. I wanted to create a place where college women could come together to find support and advice during one of the most important times of a girl's life. We worked tirelessly to recruit a group of contributors with a diverse range of experience for the book that you now hold in your hands. I want thank all of the contributors for being completely open and honest in sharing their personal stories. It is my sincere hope that what you will discover in reading *U Chic* is that we are all sisters in the end.

From Kirthana Ramisetti, managing editor, UniversityChic.com

When I became managing editor of UniversityChic.com in 2006, I had been out of college for six years. I could hazily recall memories of that time—the roommate who never left our dorm room except to go to 5 a.m. spinning classes, the *Real World* marathons that my friends and I would watch on lazy weekends, the all-night study sessions fueled by soda and Twizzlers—and so I imagined that the travails and joys I had experienced as an undergrad would be similar to that of University Chic readers and contributors.

I was right. And I was wrong. But mostly right. The world has become so much more complicated in just a few short years. When I graduated, music-sharing software was still a novelty, and people had only recently stopped worrying about the Y2K bug and the technological havoc it was supposed to wreak. Now, college students live in the post-9/11 era, a time notable for how seamlessly technology mixes with our personal and professional lives. Facebook, YouTube, and text messaging are just some of the innovations that have changed how college students represent themselves and communicate with each other. These advances are mixed blessings, opening up students' worlds in unimaginable ways, while also leaving them vulnerable to personal attacks and criticism.

Yet despite all this, I learned from my time at University Chic that college life hasn't really changed. The same anxieties and expectations that impacted previous generations still exist: *Will I be able to get along with my roommate? When should I declare a major? Should I join a sorority? How do I balance academics, work, and a social life?* The answers to all these questions and so much more can be found in this book. I was so impressed by our contributors' spark, drive, ambition, and how they strove to take advantage of all the opportunities that college has to offer them.

I really do believe there has not been a generation of college women hungrier for success, yet also more generous with their time and energy to assist those less fortunate. They are not just students at their respective schools, but students of the world— open-minded, openhearted, and open to what the future holds for them. I thank them for contributing such wonderful stories that are sure to help and inspire other women soon to follow in their footsteps.

welcome to *u chic:*
the college girl's guide to
everything!

· ·

*W*hether you're headed to college or are already there, one thing is certain: college is the time to expand your horizons. You need to experience college in *your own* way, and our guide is here to help you discover it!

With the endless choices you'll face in college, you'll often have questions and find yourself in need of a little advice. Our hope is that you find your answers here. We asked college women across the country to dish about their collegiate experiences, challenges, and successes. The result? A guide that provides you with exclusive advice that could only come from those who have experienced it for themselves. From preparing to move, to dating advice, to finding the right balance of school and fun, you will find answers and insights to your important questions in these shared experiences from college women around the country. This is a book that you can turn to throughout your entire college career. In that spirit, don't feel like you need to sit down and read the book cover-to-cover (though that certainly won't hurt anything!). Each of our contributors has answered specific questions, so you can turn right to the section you need, when you need it.

With *U Chic*, the conversation doesn't stop at the last page. Let's say you have a specific question that is not directly addressed. We've created an online chat area at UniversityChic.com exclusively for readers, where you can comment on things that you've read in the guide, seek further advice, or read more about or even contact the guide's writers. This guide is truly the start of a conversation that can last throughout your entire college career.

So what are you waiting for? Turn the page and be on your way to *your own* fabulous college experience!

xoxo,

Christie Garton

Founder, UniversityChic.com

CHAPTER 1

Getting Started

Starting to get serious about where you'd like to go to college? Or maybe you were already accepted and are packing for your new home now. Either way, this chapter has you covered. You probably are already well aware that the transition to college is a major stress. Besides maybe summer camp, when else have you packed up your entire life's belongings into several boxes and suitcases to head off to an unknown place to live with some random stranger? To help smooth your path, this chapter is filled with insider advice on making this transition with confidence and style. As Carrie Bradshaw might say, we wish we were in your Choos, starting the college experience all over again!

get over not getting into your first choice school (or second or third)

Allison Davis, Barnard College

I had known from the age of 12 that I was destined to attend Brown University. This had been decided before I had even visited the campus. I'd just read about it in one of my brother's college brochures, but regardless, I knew I was going to Brown to study theater and to be a free spirit under a requirement-free curriculum. And maybe join a naked protest or two.

Six years and a $70 application fee later, my hopes were dashed. *I didn't get in.* When I received that thin, impersonal rejection letter, I went through the Kübler-Ross cycle of grief faster than you can say "safety school." First there was denial. *No way, I totally got in; they got the wrong Allison Davis.* Then anger. *Those jerks—what do they know about college admissions?!* Followed by bargaining. *I'll retake my SATs, do 600 more hours of community service—anything!* Next, depression. *My world has ended.* And, finally, acceptance.

Did You Know?

The schools with the lowest acceptance rates are actually music schools—Philadelphia's Curtis Institute of Music and New York's Juilliard School have acceptance rates less than 8%. Harvard comes in next at 9%.

Honestly, the rejection letter stung. A lot. You spend 4+ years slaving over SATs, GPAs, APs, extracurriculars, and enough community service to be on par with a Peace Corps member just to qualify for *consideration* at your dream school—the only university or college that you fervently believe matches who you are and, more importantly, who you want to become. It's almost like an unhealthy romantic relationship; your whole self-worth becomes involved in impressing "the one." It is disappointing to be so brusquely rejected by what was your collegiate soul mate.

HOW TO COPE

So you did not get a fat acceptance package from your first choice school. Disappointing? Absolutely. But devastating? No. If you get rejected from your first (or second or third) choice school, give yourself some time to be upset, but remember there are about 6 billion different possible reasons for an admission decision. There is almost no way to understand the why, which is really frustrating. Rather than wallow over the unanswerable "why" by tearing yourself and your application apart, focus on what you do have—other college choices.

When I got my rejection letter from Brown, I cried, threw things, tore up the letter, but then I got some sanity back. Brown was 1 school out of 13 that I applied to. And at the end of the whole ordeal, I may not have gotten into Brown, but I ended up with 12 other acceptances and eventually was accepted to the school that I now proudly call my alma mater, Barnard College.

Once you've been rejected, you may feel a little lost as to what to do next. Since we can't all create our own fake colleges like Justin Long did in the movie *Accepted*, considering other *real* schools is the logical next step.

WHAT TO DO IF YOU APPLIED EARLY DECISION

If you applied early decision, or early action, and didn't make it in, go talk to the college counselor at your high school. You have a nice stretch of time to reconsider schools and find new ones. Before you go, make a list of the reasons you fell in love with First Choice University. Was it the rural environment? The ivy-covered brick buildings? The out-of-this-world biochemistry department? Well, guess what? Other campuses have the same things. Your college counselor can help you find other schools with similar criteria and whose admissions standards more closely fit what you have to offer.

Something else to consider is the *tabula rasa* approach to looking for new schools. By weighing your original reasons for choosing your first choice school, you also have a second chance to evaluate what you actually want out of a college. In high school, especially, it is so easy to be pushed into a neat little box with a concise label. I'm sure you can hear it now: you are "the really athletic girl" or "the really brainy girl." But maybe there is another girl inside you that you need to explore. College gives you that opportunity. Consider applying to a school that has what you know you are interested in (like a good badminton team) but may also have a strong reputation in something you want to pursue in the future.

A WHOLE NEW SET OF POSSIBILITIES

I always considered myself the quirky, alternative-theater girl. I thought I wanted to be in a small town where most of your life revolved around the campus. I also wanted a campus with a strong academic history and, yes, with ivy-covered buildings. Once I didn't get into Brown, I considered other schools just like it—Vassar and Bowdoin were my next top candidates. My college counselor reminded me that I was an active writer and that maybe I should consider schools that had strong writing programs. It was a great suggestion. I had always intended to go to school for theater—something that I had done almost my entire life. But by expanding my college search to those with well-known writing programs, I began to see a whole new set of options, and what I had thought I had wanted out of a school changed. Suddenly, I was attracted to schools in bigger cities, like Barnard. And though I still have my ivy-covered buildings, campus life is no longer the focal point of my social activities. Truly, Barnard helped me discover my real passion and develop into a person I didn't even know I could be. And maybe this would have happened at Vassar or Bowdoin as well, but the reevaluations I did during my second admissions process opened a lot of possibilities.

FOR REGULAR DECISION APPLICANTS

If you applied regular decision and didn't get in, you'll have other admissions decisions coming at the same time, meaning there are likely several acceptance letters to look forward to. Even though you really wanted to go to First Choice University, there were

U Chic Tip!

Once you find a school (or schools) you want to apply to, go back to your college counselor and ask for application hints. For instance, let's say that you play varsity lacrosse during your four years of high school but you also sing in the chorale. Your college counselor can help you work both of those unique experiences into your personal essay. Or maybe you'll find that your application is perfect already, but chances are, with a reevaluation and some helpful hints from your high school's resident college expert, you can find some way to better your chances for the second round of applications.

reasons you liked all the other schools you applied to. Go back and reconsider those reasons. If you have the time, go spend a weekend at one or two of the schools that are your remaining top choices. The most important thing to remember is to stop comparing it to First Choice University. It's fine to say, "Well, I really liked how that school had eco-friendly dorms." But if you are comparing the linoleum of the dorm room floors, you are setting yourself up for disappointment in the end. Look at the positive aspects of each school rather than considering what it doesn't have.

I know it's cheesy to remind you of the old saying that you'll end up where you were meant to be, but it's kind of true. Somehow, even if the school you end up going to isn't the one you thought you wanted, it may end up being the best fit.

FINAL THOUGHTS

After three years at Barnard, I knew that I loved where I was, but I always wondered, "What if I had gone to Brown?" Well, I went to visit a friend of mine who attends Brown last year. The campus was as beautiful as I had remembered. Providence is a great town, and I really liked the people. But there was something missing for me this time I went back. If I had gone to Brown, I never would have been able to take a writing class where Rachel Weiss made an appearance so we could learn the art of interviewing. I would never have been able to spend my semesters interning at the *New York Times*, and I would not have been able to hop on a subway and see a Tony-winning play and then come back to campus and hang out at a dorm party later in the evening. I would have missed out on so many different and wonderful opportunities.

And the funny part of this story is that my friend who goes to Brown chose it because she hadn't gotten into Columbia University in New York City. After I had been going on and on about how much I loved going to school in the city and how much I love Barnard, she said, "If I had gone to Columbia, I would have been lost. Brown was such a better fit." So, case in point: sometimes the things we ask for aren't really the things we need. If your first choice university took a pass, be grateful because your second (or third or fourth) choice will most likely be the better choice in the end.

how to survive and thrive
when in the minority

Emily Kaplan, University of California – Davis

Growing up in a small town where every fourth name in the school directory was Feldman or Cohen, it is easy to assume that being Jewish is just as common as having brown hair. But you know what they say about assuming things: it's bad. So when you finally hit college—an overwhelming occasion in itself—what do you do when you find out how very much in the minority you may be?

DON'T PANIC
First of all, don't panic. Check out opportunities on campus. Attend new student fairs and collect pamphlets, or go to the student life office on campus where you'll find lists of clubs and organizations. And let us not forget, the mother of all information sources—Facebook. From the local Temple to Hillel (the largest Jewish student organization in the world), there were plenty of

Judaism-affiliated opportunities for me at UC–Davis to choose from. Bottom line: All I had to do was look around.

Why I Chose a Historically Black College or University

Briana Peppers, Spelman College

What I love most about attending a black college is that I can be whoever I desire to be. I can embrace any style or social outlet wholeheartedly and be welcomed. In fact, when it comes to personal style, the more different, the better. I exit my residence hall to regularly see hairstyles from the '80s paired with classic pearls and '70s dress. On other days, I exit my residence hall to see suits and laptops. For the males, it's not uncommon to see the bowtie, and I absolutely love it! It is, indeed, a southern gentleman's necessity. What I'm referring to here is more than just fashion. The style reflects a deeper truth in that the students are always so poised and well versed. They are genuine "renaissance" women and men. I knew that I wanted to earn the same title. I wanted to be refined and perfected. This is what compelled me most to attend Spelman College.

What to expect

Overall, life at a black college can be described as peaceful hysteria. It is full of constant excitement and passion but also so comforting and needed. To make things even more exciting, a social or academic event is always going on at a black college. Every Friday, Spelman hosts an outdoor celebration complete with music and food and vendors. We call it Market Friday.

Another great aspect of the HBCU experience are the experiences and traditions that are specific to black colleges. For example, every year during freshman orientation each member of the freshman class must experience an "initiation" into the Spelman sisterhood. I am not referring to anything dangerous or illegal. I am only referring to a memory that links every Spelman student and every Spelman woman together!

There really is genuine sisterhood and brotherhood. The bond is somewhat like being in a sorority or fraternity without the pledging and initiation process. No matter what stage you are at in life, there will always be a group of people everywhere—ranging in all ages and social hierarchies—that are willing to give their last to you just because you, too, are a student or alumni of their alma mater. What I'm referring to is also about being a family. Just saying the name of the school can immediately turn a stranger into a family member. For example, a Spelman alumna once told me how she actually chased a vehicle with a Spelman College sticker just so she could say hello. Once she got close, filled with excitement, she jumped out of her own car to shout, "My Sister!"

Be prepared for a challenge

Students in a black college must be ready to combat the belief that our education is not as challenging as other college academic programs. It most definitely is. Our academics are equally as challenging and serve as an equivalent preparation for life.

What is different are the unique academic offerings that you'll find at an HBCU. A black college is one of the few places where knowledge and empowerment can come from titles such as *Gender as Analytical Category* by Beverly Guy-Sheftall or Aimé Césaire's *Discourse on Colonialism*. This knowledge is a rarity and a treasure. We are so fortunate at HBCUs for this enlightenment to be our foundation. When I was a senior in high school, a recruiter from Tuskegee University shared this fact with me. At the time, I understood the message, but now, attending Spelman, I understand its truth.

There is something really unique and special about students at an HBCU that no one adjective can pinpoint. The one thing that binds us together the most is not race but our potential and vision. Some may argue that all college students are bound for something great in their future. This is probably true, but the future for students in Historically Black Colleges and Universities is more than a future. It is a destiny. Everything we do is powerful. Your time in a Historically Black College or University will be incredible! There is a persona and a mystique that will be with you forever, and it cannot be found anywhere else. So welcome. We are waiting.

SHOW UP

As lame as it sounds to be the new kid in five different clubs, sometimes just showing up will demonstrate that you are really serious about making connections. Go somewhere and join something that is related to your religion or ethnic heritage. When I went to my first sorority recruitment event, I had no clue that sorority membership would help me connect to the Jewish community at my school.

Nevertheless, I wound up attending Friday night services once a month (which I had never done before), hosted my own Shabbat dinners, and did much more for the Jewish community than I'd ever done before in my life. And now, I'm the president of a Jewish-interest sorority. Go figure.

REMEMBER, MINORITY DOESN'T MEAN LONELY

It can be hard being in the minority for any reason—political, ethnic, or religious. But remember that even though you're not the majority, that does not mean you are alone. Think about it this way: if all the minorities got together, we would likely rival the majority. Take solace in that fact, and remember that if you're feeling alone, someone else is probably feeling the same. Perhaps you can help each other out so that neither of you have to be sad in your perceived solitude.

HAVE FAITH

When it comes to surviving and thriving, being yourself is the only thing to hold on to. If your beliefs come under siege, having faith is mandatory. People can try to threaten your beliefs through hurtful words, vandalism, or just general meanness. I wish I could say that never happens, but it does. However, no one can take away your beliefs or your sense of self worth. End of story.

Staying True to Your Roots

Raneisha Williams, Ripon College

"Our lives begin to end the day we become silent about the things that matter."

—Martin Luther King Jr.

The instant I set foot on campus my first day in college, I could hardly believe what I had gotten myself into. I was truly in the minority—an African American female on a predominantly white campus. I knew that this would be outside my comfort zone. But my desire to learn encouraged me to conquer any fears that I had about going. I simply wanted a good education. Certainly, I have come across racial stereotypes along the way. However, what I've found is that those generalizations are based on ignorance rather than hate. Instead of getting upset those times when people have questioned my abilities or counted me out, I have worked harder to prove myself. This means that I always have to be on my toes, but the funny thing is, I have been doing that my whole life.

So here I am, and I'm not backing down. Instead of accepting how things currently are, I am constantly searching for ways to alleviate racial tension and discrepancies. And, because of this, I feel powerful. If you're in a similar situation, it's completely normal to feel that people may not quite understand where you're coming from at times. But if you stay true to yourself, work hard, and make an effort to educate others about where you come from and how *you* see things, you are taking the best steps forward in getting a great education while helping educate the world.

AND JUST REMEMBER...

If it's important to you, don't lose sight of your identity. Hang on to your values, your traditions, and the connections that you have to your religion and heritage. Create your own community, whether that means joining an existing one or starting from scratch.

put an end to homesickness!

Allison Davis, Barnard College

I fear change—and college is a big change. So it was no surprise that I spent the majority of my summer before college *freaking out* about the thought of being in a new place without my friends, without my boyfriend, without my family. As if preparing for a coming storm, I went around buying everything that I could think of to start a "home" emergency kit—a stash of items that would remind me of home when I was stuck in a tiny dorm room. Why wouldn't I? In my mind, the dorm was that weird place that conjured up images of girls-gone-wild meets summer camp. I even went so far as to ask my mother to get custom-made bedding inspired by my bedding at home. Sadly, she declined, so to cope I instead bought dorm accessories with the same purple and gold color scheme as my childhood bedroom.

Well, despite all of my numerous breakdowns in the Target store, my first week of college was fine. I think I even had fun during first week's orientation! The wonderful thing about orientation is that they keep you busy with so many activities that you forget to be homesick. And most of these activities are the special kind of lame that have you instantly bonding with members of your orientation group just to survive. Voila! Instant friendships.

AFTER THE FIRST WEEK

But the real challenge during your transition to college is after orientation—your first unstructured weekend. I almost couldn't handle it. Who was I supposed to hang out with? These people weren't really my friends; I'd known them for only five days! And communal bathrooms? I was so over it after the first time some random guy caught me shaving my legs in the sink.

I just wanted to go home and see my best friend, watch a movie with my boyfriend, and pee in the privacy of my own bathroom. Between you and me, I almost did. I was about 5 minutes away from booking a train ticket home for the first weekend when I gave myself a pause. I realized that if I went running for the comforts of suburbia every time things became uncomfortable, I'd spend my college experience in a friendless black hole with nothing but my books to keep me company. So, against my instincts to cut and run, I decided to stay. Looking back, that decision was the best one I have made over the course of my 4 years at school. In fact, I met some of the girls who would become my best friends at school that weekend.

Renee and I were both terminally bored at a tropically themed Alpha Epsilon Pi frat party (read: warm jungle juice and underdeveloped shirtless frat boys). We both decided to leave the party in exchange for a band's live show elsewhere on campus. That was one of the best nights of my college career. After that, Renee and I started going out to events that interested us rather than the ones that felt "college-y," and eventually found a lot of people were interested in doing the same. Once I started finding things I liked to do and inviting people, I made friends.

Once I started making more friends and building a life by taking risks and going out with new people, the homesickness went away. If you're concerned that you may, too, experience a difficult transition, there are several things you can do to make the transition a little bit easier and get yourself out of the funk a little bit faster.

And communal bathrooms? I was so over it after the first time some random guy caught me shaving my legs in the sink.

TRY SOME PREEMPTIVE PEP TALK

Just take a deep breath and accept it: you are probably going to get homesick. It may vary in degrees of awfulness, but at some point, you are going to miss the people and places that you encountered every day for the past 18 years. Don't suppress these feelings: it's completely natural and pretty common. If you go into college thinking you are never going to miss anyone or anything, you are setting yourself up for a fall and may be caught off guard, unable to deal with the unexpected sad feelings. By taking the time to accept the fact that you may get lonely or begin to miss home a time or two, you can prepare yourself rather than being surprised by these feelings of homesickness. It may be hard to deal with these emotions, but it isn't impossible. This preemptive pep talk goes a long way.

IT'S OK TO BRING THINGS THAT REMIND YOU OF HOME, BUT DON'T BRING *HOME*

Sure, bring a few pictures of your friends and family, your favorite stuffed animal, and maybe even a special tchotchke. (The ceramic pony my dad gave me when I was 7 will always be on my desk regardless of what anyone says.) They are even good conversation starters. It makes complete sense that you want to surround yourself with familiar things, but there is a limit to how much. Filling up your new space with remnants of the past makes it really difficult to enjoy the present. (Plus your roommate may not appreciate all your trinkets from home.) It is probably not a good idea to bring all of your yearbooks from high school, your collection of sweatshirts from old boyfriends, or that sweater you haven't worn since you were 7 but you *swear* you can still smell your first grade teacher's perfume on it.

You're in college to make new memories and develop into a

well-rounded person. How to do this? Make sure your 8 x 10-foot cell of a dorm room has space for your new life. It will fill up before you know it.

> It is probably not a good idea to bring all of your yearbooks from high school, your collection of sweatshirts from old boyfriends, or that sweater you haven't worn since you were 7 but you swear you can still smell your first grade teacher's perfume on it.

GET YOURSELF OUT THERE

It may be easier to go to bed early or spend hours in the library in order to get ahead in your classes, and these are good habits in most cases, but taking it to the extreme can lead to a dangerous pattern. Even worse, you could have done the very same thing at home! You're ignoring the perks and pleasures of college life, and that's not healthy.

Take advantage of being in college by seizing those opportunities to socialize and meet people you would not have met otherwise. It might feel like you're putting yourself out on the line by trying to hang out with new people, so to make it easier, simply join a new club, write for the student newspaper, or strike up a conversation with someone in your freshman seminar course. What do you have to lose? For the first few weeks, everyone is looking to make friends, so people will be receptive. After you introduce yourself, it's only awkward for the first few minutes of conversation, or until you find out that Sarah in your Intro to Poli Sci course also shares your love of obscure Austrian electro hip hop.

Once you start talking, you'll be amazed at how much you have in common with and have to learn from the new people around you.

> After you introduce yourself, it's only awkward for the first few minutes of conversation, or until you find out that Sarah in your Intro to Poli Sci course also shares your love of obscure Austrian electro hip hop.

KEEP IN TOUCH WITH FRIENDS AND FAMILY, BUT TO A REASONABLE DEGREE

Thanks to the communication age we live in, you can call, text, email, instant message, Skype, or Facebook all the people you left behind for hours on end. But try not to. It's hard at first, but spending hours talking to people via whatever your preferred communication method might mean that you are losing precious hours of face-to-face conversation with people at your college. A good rule of thumb: until you have started building a niche for yourself at school, avoid spending more time talking to people from home than you do talking to your classmates.

My freshman-year roommate talked to her boyfriend for about 8 hours a day. I really wasn't surprised when she transferred to her boyfriend's college after first semester because she felt so alone.

It makes it harder to create a home at school when you're constantly talking to people from home. Plus your best friend is trying to make friends at her own school, so give her—and yourself—a chance to create a new life for yourselves at college.

U Chic Tip! Relying on Old and New Friends
Melanie Harris, Virginia Tech

Let's say that you're having a difficult time and need to chat with your old friends for some support. Go for it. Don't hesitate to call your besties from high school, but do so only when you need to or have something particularly great to share—definitely not every day. I can't emphasize enough how important it is to work on building a new life, and you can't move on when you're too much in touch with your old pals. And really, it's not fair to be calling or texting them all the time.

As an alternative to calling old friends *all* the time, reach out to your new friends. The National Mental Health Association encourages students to seek support from a roommate or a friend from class. Friendships can help make a strange place feel more friendly and comfortable. Sharing your emotions reduces isolation and helps you realize that you are not alone. This way, you're working on making a new life for yourself and moving on in a healthy way. Before you know it, these new bonds and connections will change your whole outlook on the college experience for the better, and your old friends might happily end up wondering why you're not calling as often as you used to.

REALIZE THAT MOST STUDENTS ARE GOING THROUGH THE SAME THING

It may seem like everyone is having an easier time making friends and having a life than you—but they aren't. Most of the time, people like to act like they're partying every night and have thousands of friends. This is actually a fact you may learn in your first psychology course—if you act popular, people are more likely to perceive you as popular. But deep down, everyone feels a little lost and alone at the start of school. It's just that people show it in different ways. If you are feeling really alone, reach out to someone—your roommate or a hall-mate—and say, "I'm feeling a little alone. How are you coping with all of this?" If you think that is lame, just take solace in the fact that everybody is feeling a little disoriented and may appreciate the opportunity to share their feelings. I guarantee that you will quickly discover that you are not the only one feeling alone. Think of it this way: if someone confided their feelings, you would hear them out without hesitation.

GET SOME STRUCTURE

The first week of college feels like a scene out of *Camp Nowhere* where everyone can run around and do whatever they want, whenever they want. That's kind of cool after having your life scheduled down to the minute in high school. But trust me: it takes almost a week, but this kind of freedom does lose its novelty. Don't forget that your goal is to build a life at school, not to become a professional spring-breaker. Once you start classes, join clubs, become active, and find people to join you at the dining hall, you'll find that all these things require a schedule, and a structured schedule is your best friend. You'll waste hours wondering what you are going to do and who you are going to do it with if you're not careful, so embrace your fabulously busy life with a fabulous schedule.

STAY TRUE TO YOURSELF

There are some tempting shortcuts to getting over homesickness, including things like drinking a lot, sleeping with random boys, or joining the chess club even though it bores you to tears. In short, it is easy to silence who you really are for the sake of having companions. But remember, if you build false relationships now, they won't last, and you'll find yourself lonely again. It may suck to feel alone during the early stages, but it's going to suck more when you find yourself friendless at the end of second semester because you feigned an interest in being in a sorority. Or conversely, you shunned sororities because a friend told you to, even though you knew it was right for you. Take the time to build true friendships that are based on your real interests at the very beginning of school. I promise it will pay off later.

U Chic Tip! Care Packages Go a Long Way

My mom sends me care packages for everything; it has been the one saving grace of my college experience. I went to London to study abroad for a semester and she sent me packages filled with Oreos and American peanut butter. I was the most popular Yank in my flat! If you are feeling sad, ask your parents for a care package—it's a nice way to be reminded that people out there love you. And offers of your mom's chocolate chunk cookies are great icebreakers for making new friends.

TRY NOT TO GO OVERBOARD

For every girl who thinks staying in her room doing nothing is the best way to cure homesickness, there will be another that has to join every club, get every person's number, and knock on everyone's door. Don't be that girl. She generally ends up burned-out and friendless because she annoys people. It is great to put yourself out there to make a big network of friends and activities, but don't force it to happen right away. Bottom line: it's about the quality, not quantity, of friendships. So what if you only play one sport or only have one or two really good friends at first? If these friends are fun and worth your time, you only need a few. And definitely don't worry about winning any popularity contest. By the end of college you will have tons of friends and way too many activities; just give it time.

IF IT DOESN'T GET BETTER, TALK TO A COUNSELOR

There is a difference between being a little (or even a lot) sad about missing home and being depressed. If months go by and you still really hate school, your grades suffer, you can't stop crying, and you sleep too much or not enough, go talk to someone. There are counseling centers on every college campus that are there to help students cope with homesickness or any other issues on your mind. Going to college means a lot of new and wonderful opportunities, but it also means a lot of changes that we aren't always equipped to handle.

If you are lucky enough to never be homesick, I certainly envy you. But if you are, these tips are a surefire way to beat homesickness. Once you do that, you're ready for four unforgettable years.

U Chic Essentials—Getting Started

Stay true to yourself

It is tempting to silence who you really are for the sake of having companions. But remember, if you build false relationships now, they won't last, and you'll find yourself lonely again.

Limit too much contact with your past

Until you have started building a niche for yourself at school, avoid spending more time talking to people from home than your new classmates.

Get some structure

The best remedy for homesickness? Getting out and getting involved. As soon as you hit the campus pavement, start looking for opportunities to get involved and meet new people. And before you know it, there won't be any time in your schedule to miss home.

Looking for more great advice? Head to www.UniversityChic.com and look for "U Chic Picks!" for our fav resources and websites—they come highly recommended from our guide's contributors and editors. Be sure to leave your suggestions as well!

CHAPTER 2

Sharing Space

The previous chapter was all about making the transition to college. In this chapter, our writers dish on another early-stage college experience—sharing space with a roommate. Sharing a room in the dorms—especially when the room is an itty-bitty hole in the wall—is no easy feat. For those of you who were privileged with pimped-out bedrooms and private baths back home, get ready for a change. Before you even arrive, common questions you may face include: Should I room with my BFF from high school? What if my roommate is a freak? Where do I find extra-long bed sheets? Are coed dorms the way to go? Is the scholarship hall or sorority house for me? It's normal to have all of these concerns and questions when it comes to sharing space.

Here's the low-down on how to "live it up" in college no matter what your living situation may be.

bringing some sanity to dorm-room chaos

Anna Prestek, University of Washington—Seattle

When you're entering college as a freshman, it can seem that the classes and the countless hours studying, preparing presentations, and writing papers are the defining focal points of your new life. But an equally important part of the college experience involves your living situation. Whether you're required to live in a dorm as a first-year student or you opt for off-campus housing, here's some advice on how to manage dorm-room chaos while making the best out of any living situation.

CONTACT YOUR ROOMMATE-TO-BE

Many colleges will allow you to choose your roommate ahead of time—like your best friend from high school who's attending the same college. This may seem like a no-brainer. But a word of advice here: while choosing to live with a current friend can be a good choice because she's someone you already know and love (it's comfortable!), living with someone that you've never met can be a great way to become exposed to an entirely new set of friends.

I didn't have many high school friends who were going to the same college, so I opted to allow the university to choose a roommate for me. My new roommate, Grace, was completely different from me in family background, music tastes, clothing, and pretty much everything else under the sun. At first, I was worried that we wouldn't get along, considering my abiding love of Britney Spears and celebrity gossip websites and her complete distaste for these "frivolous" things. But for the most part, it was a great experience. Yes, she liked to listen to the Aquabats and hang slides from her presentation on leprosy in our window, but these initial annoyances taught me to be tolerant of others and be open to someone else's tastes. Because I kept an open mind, I was exposed to films, music, and people I would probably never have encountered if left to my own devices. Since she was a junior—a couple years older than me—Grace was also a good source of information on important things, from where to grab a bite on campus to negotiating the vast library system. She was virtually a stranger to me when we met, but over time and with an open mind, we came to enjoy each other's company.

For those of you who decide to live with someone entirely new, your college will usually send you the contact information for your new roomie and vice versa. A great way to break the ice is to give her a call before you even arrive on campus. Introduce yourself and find out what each of your expectations are for living together. This is also a great chance to get to know each other.

A FEW THINGS TO CONSIDER ASKING YOUR ROOMIE-TO-BE

- **When is she planning to move in?** It might be a good idea to coordinate your move on the same day, as this prevents one person from claiming their part of the room without consulting the other. Also, the two of you can configure the furniture and decorate the room in a way that is mutually acceptable.

- **Is she a morning person or a night owl?** Differences in sleeping schedules can pose a problem when on the first night you find out that she keeps the lights blazing 'til 1 a.m. and you're in bed by 9 p.m. sharp. Knowing her personal schedule beforehand can prevent an unexpected surprise when it's time to get some shut-eye. Consider buying a sleep mask and some high-quality earplugs. These can block the light of your roomie's desk lamp and the "ping" of her instant messaging when you're trying to catch some much-needed z's.

- **Would she like to grab coffee or lunch the first day you meet?** If you can't move in on the same day, no worries. As soon as the dust settles, invite your roommate to go to coffee, have lunch, or just take a walk through campus. By making an effort to get to know her, you show that you care about being a good roommate and possibly even friends.

KNOW AND MAKE KNOWN YOUR BOUNDARIES

So you've moved in your stuff and shared some pizza slices and a chat. But what happens when you discover some red flags about your roommate? Maybe you find out that she has a long-term boyfriend who's big on PDA and wants to hang in your room on a nightly basis. Or does she listen to Evergreen Terrace and Avenged Sevenfold while you're an Alicia Keys and Sara Bareilles fan? Worst-case scenario: she's allowing drugs or alcohol in the room and, through guilt by association, you could potentially get in trouble.

Though you generally can't control what other people do, being clear about what is or isn't acceptable will make it easier for you to voice your opinions without having to second-guess yourself.

U Chic Tip! Your RA Is Your Best Ally

If drugs are involved, go speak with your Resident Assistant immediately. These things are illegal, and you should not have to put up with them.

SPEAK UP

Something is bothering you, but where to begin? Start by speaking up. Your roommate may not have any idea that what she's doing is bothering you. Some people simply have a higher threshold as to what is acceptable behavior around others. She might not think having her friend lean his greasy bike against your bed frame is offensive, while you may be deeply disturbed. If you feel uncomfortable with something that's happening, let your roommate know. Don't be afraid that you're being inconsiderate by voicing your concerns. It's like that one famous line in a wedding ceremony: "Speak now or forever hold your peace." Think about it: there's never a "right" time to bring up a topic that's bothering you. But trust me: it'll usually go better if you speak your mind from the beginning, rather than suffering in silence and having that influence your attitude toward her.

COME PREPARED

Since you're sharing a room, each inhabitant is entitled to equal space in said room. However, dorm rooms, being as small as they are, become even smaller once you move in TVs, microwaves, stereo systems, and minifridges. Be considerate of your roommate by not taking up too much of the communal floor space. If you have a bike, store it in a bike room to keep your bedroom clear and prevent dirt from tracking in. Put your laundry basket on top of your closet if there's space, or under your bed.

U Chic Tips for Dorm-Room Bliss!

Tip 1: Must-have furnishings

There are just some things you do not want to neglect bringing, including: a file cabinet or several storage bins to keep your papers organized; a rug for those cold dorm-room floors; and tall shelves so you can store a lot without taking up space.

Tip 2: A comfortable bed makes for a comfortable room

You must get extra-long twin sheets. That's the number-one rule for dorm-room bedding because dorm-room beds are notorious for being extra-long. Also, bring several sets of sheets. There will be times when you want clean sheets at 2 a.m. but are obviously not in the mood to do the laundry. Finally, a mattress pad will ensure your much-needed beauty rest.

Tip 3: Utilize every inch of space

Consider lofting your bed. You can usually get lofting kits from maintenance or the front desk of your residence hall. When finished, the area under your bed can become a great place for a comfy chair and a reading lamp, creating another sitting area besides your bed and desk. To additionally free up some space, add hooks to the backs of doors. You'll be surprised how an extra towel or two on the ground can really detract from the room's overall good vibe.

Tip 4: Go green!

If protecting the environment is of concern to you (of course it is!), you can introduce eco-friendliness to your dorm room through green

....

furniture, a recycling bin, and energy-saving items like compact
fluorescent lightbulbs.

....

If you opt for a shared fridge, make sure you don't take up
more than your half. Free up even more space by foregoing items
like microwaves and mini-ironing boards. Many dorms have
kitchenettes on each floor that contain essentials such as microwaves,
sinks, ovens, and ironing boards. You can also make an impromptu
ironing board by putting a towel on your bed. Basically, it all boils
down to coming prepared and being resourceful. Only bring items
into the dorm room that you know you will use, and if you're in
doubt, leave it at home. It can always be shipped to you later or
you can get it during a visit home over the holidays. Space is at a
premium, so pack light and enjoy your clutter-free environs.

I also recommend making your toiletries as easy to carry as
possible by investing in a good shower caddy with holes for water
to drain. I made the mistake of buying one that didn't have holes
in the bottom, causing water to puddle in the bottom and mold
until I had to stab a hole in it myself with a pair of scissors. Also,
consider decanting your shampoo, conditioner, body wash, and the
like into travel-size bottles. This will lighten your load considerably
when you're making morning and nightly treks to the bathroom.

UTILIZE OTHER AREAS

So you've talked to your roommate and have made sure that
everything fits in your tiny living space. But what to do when there

are times when she has unexpected guests over? That's one of the great and, at times, most irritating things about the dorms: you're constantly surrounded by people. Certainly, there will be times when you or your roommate will want to invite others to your room to watch movies, eat, or just hang out. This is fine until the day comes when you have to study for an exam and your roommate and her four closest friends want to play *Guitar Hero*. This is a perfect time to check out the other amenities your dorm has to offer. Some dorms have study rooms, usually a windowless room set up with a table and a chair where you can take your laptop and books to read or write in solitude. Maybe there's a lounge on your floor with couches and tables where you can study in relative peace and quiet. Keep in mind, though, since it's a shared space, you may have to vacate if a group decides they want to watch TV.

OTHER AMENITIES TO CONSIDER

Don't forget that you can always leave the dorm and check out a library on campus. Many schools have at least one library that's open late or even 24 hours. If you go after dark, stay safe by taking the bus or call campus security and have someone come and escort you to your destination. Another reason to get out of the dorm: sometimes all you need is a break from your roommate and from your regular surroundings to reset your outlook. We all have to take a break from others at times, even the people we love the most.

When all is said and done, there are going to be moments of great fun and frivolity in dorm life and also some frenzy and frustration, too. Knowing and accepting this ahead of time will make the transition to dorm living a whole lot easier than coming unprepared. Expect that there will be some situations that may catch you off guard or test your annoyance threshold, but overall, the dorm can be a great place to make friends and lay your head down at night.

a fashionista's tips
on fitting it all in

Alyssa Vande Leest, University of Wisconsin

How do you fit a roomful of clothing, shoes, and accessories into a tiny 4 x 3-foot cube? No, it isn't a riddle or a math problem, it's the dilemma faced by every fashion-loving college-bound student. Unless you've been blessed with living accommodations that provide you with the luxury of a walk-in closet—and if you have, I seriously doubt you're at college—you face the task of devising a plan to keep your clothes from overflowing into your tiny dorm room or apartment. You need to stock it with the essentials that keep you looking fashionable and fresh, essentials that are practical for both your climate and your busy life as a college student.

Read on to find several easy tips for evaluating your style. Knowing exactly what you like will help you decide what's essential to have in your tiny room and what can be left behind, while at the same time keeping your wardrobe in top shape.

TIP 1: RECOGNIZE THAT YOU CAN'T TAKE IT ALL

I know, it's tough, but unless you've already pared your wardrobe down to favorites and essentials, there's no way you're going to fit every pair of jeans, every purse, or every shoe into your new closet. Some things are going to have to stay behind. But fear not: the next couple steps will help you to make wise decisions about what to bring and what to leave behind.

TIP 2: LIST YOUR FAVORITES

Make a short list of the items in your closet that you turn to again and again, the ones you love to wear. My list includes such things as a plain white peasant top from American Eagle, my black Puma yoga pants, a chunky cream-colored cardigan, my dark skinny jeans, and a pair of chocolate ballet flats, to name a few. Keep your list short, but honest: try to include the things you actually wear often (and not ones you keep meaning to wear often…), and make sure you include items that work together in different combinations to make a wide array of outfits. Finally, classify each favorite by the season in which you would wear it—you can swap out wardrobes for summer and winter—and make sure you've included at least a few seasonless items.

TIP 3: LIST YOUR NECESSITIES

These are the things you wear because you have to: plain black, white, tan, and brown camis, workout clothes, sweats for lazy days, and the obvious socks, underwear, and bras. Depending on where you're going to school, you may also need boots and a winter coat.

TIP 4: EVALUATE YOUR STYLE

Look at your list of favorites and think about the things you wear every day. Women in their late teens and early twenties often do not have a single, developed style and instead toy with various trends and looks, but identifying patterns in the way you dress will make it easier to choose other items to complement those favorites and necessities with old clothes and new. After you identify some of your patterns, try writing a short explanation of your style or making a collage of pictures from magazines and the Internet. This will not only provide some guidance as you expand your list and shop for new items, but may also spark new ideas on how to wear old items as the school year goes on.

TIP 5: GO SHOPPING!

Now that you know what necessities and favorites you'll be bringing along, and have an idea of the sort of style you are aiming for, it's time to go shopping. This may seem counterintuitive as most college living arrangements provide little space for clothing, but shopping smart will actually allow you to bring less, buy less later, and look better more often.

Look for gaps in your lists and fill them with versatile items that fit into the style you're going for. Personally, I'm lacking in the dressy-top department, especially when it comes to fall and winter pieces, and could use a few new pairs of comfortable walking shoes. I will definitely stock up on these things and will look for items that fit into the new earthy, richly detailed style I seem to be gravitating toward lately.

I'll also look for items that will complement those things I'm already sure to bring and wear—things like neutral-colored cardigans and shrugs, simple silver jewelry, and leather belts that will keep the same outfits looking new and fresh, even if I have to repeat them twice in one week. If you're on a budget or just want to save some money (we are college students, after all), check out stores like TJ Maxx, Filene's Basement, or Saks Off 5th, where great deals and unique pieces can always be found.

TIP 6: PLAN FOR THE SEASONS

If you're attending a school in a climate where you'll see all four seasons, you'll need to plan accordingly. However, if you will be making it home during or before Thanksgiving break, this may not be a horrible problem. Pack those things that you would wear in summer and early fall—and a few warmer items—along with a winter coat in case temperatures drop early. But plan to switch your warmer weather clothes out for your winter ones when you return home in November.

If you're far away from Mom and Dad's house, consider setting aside your cool-weather clothes and arrange to have your parents ship them to you at a certain date, at which time you'll ship back some of the lighter things you'll no longer need. If neither of these things seems to be an option, Space Bags (www.spacebag.com) can be a good alternative for storing bulky things like coats and sweaters until they are needed.

TIP 7: GET THE GEAR

Finding a way to utilize your closet space is essential when living in a dorm or apartment. Before you head off to school, consider picking up a second rod for your closet (it hangs from the built-in rod and doubles your hanging space), a belt hanger (doubles as a purse hanger), quality plastic-tube hangers, and a hanging shoe rack. Also, make sure you check with your school as to what sort of drawer space you'll be provided. Plastic drawer towers can be a great addition or alternative to a traditional dresser.

TIP 8: LEARN BY TRIAL AND ERROR

Even with the amount of planning I put into my college wardrobe before moving into my dorm, I still ended up overpacking and devoting a significant space in my 4 x 8-foot closet to clothes I didn't wear all semester.

Many of us, myself included, are chronic overpackers, exceeding the weight limit on our bags every time we fly even if we're just taking a five-day vacation. For people like us, entirely avoiding the curse of too many clothes may not be possible, but this general rule of thumb will help us overpackers stay on track: if it's too much to fit in the trunk of a normal-sized car (not a station wagon or

SUV), it's probably too much. After seeing my roommate's family's eyes pop when my dad carried my clothes from our car to my dorm room, I realized I should have adhered a bit more strongly to this rule.

Even those who don't overpack are still likely to end up with at least a few items that never get worn. Many girls change their style a bit after spending a few weeks or months on campus, and some (like myself) simply realize that those cute leather flats aren't friendly to their feet during their daily treks to class. You'll learn what works and what doesn't as the year goes on, and when it becomes clear that an item has lost its place in your closet, you have several options. If it's possible, send whatever you aren't wearing at school home. You can also consider trading unwanted items with other girls in your dorm, or sending them off to a thrift store. If you're getting rid of brand-name clothing that is still in good condition, you may be able to find a resale or consignment shop that will either pay you for your used clothing or allow you to buy space to sell it within their store and make a little money off your oldies but goodies.

The more time you spend at college, the more you'll start to understand your college style, and the easier it will become to figure out what you truly need and what you can trash.

And with a little planning and creativity, you'll be able to create a college wardrobe that meets your lifestyle needs and keeps you looking stylish, even when space is limited.

sloppy roommates? simple solutions

Katie Reynolds, Central Connecticut State University

We've all dealt (or will soon deal!) with messy living quarters—overflowing trash cans, mildew-ridden shower floors, piled-high plates in the kitchen sink. Whether your freshman roommate was randomly chosen by the school or you live with your best friend who turns out to be a total slob, messy roommates can really ruin a room's mood and possibly ruin friendships if not dealt with properly. And aside from the strain that messiness can put on relationships, it can really affect your schoolwork thanks to its drain on your motivation to stay organized.

MAKING THE MOST OF COMMUNAL LIVING AREAS

Learning to cope with other people's lifestyles is one of the major stresses you'll face during your transition to college. Start out by agreeing on some rules and making sure that everyone is clear on how the communal space should look. My senior-year suite had one bathroom, a living room, and three very tiny bedrooms for six girls. The word "messy" was an understatement. The first weekend, we each had our own idea of "fun" in the suite. Before heading out to the bar, Tracy and I decided to have our friends over for a party. Our other roommate, "Denise," was a little less enthusiastic about our fun, and I guess I can't blame her. The littered floor and the loud music coming from our bedroom probably did not make for a welcoming first weekend for her. Needless to say, Denise called a suite meeting soon after to go over some "ground rules." The meeting caught me off guard, because the last thing I wanted was someone telling me how to live. But once it started, I realized it was a positive thing for all of us.

First, each person got a chance to share their pet peeves no matter how silly they sounded to say out loud, and then we discussed ways to avoid each other's pet peeves. One roommate, "Jesse," had a real pet peeve about the trash not being emptied in a timely manner. Funny, though, we quickly learned that trash was the *least* of our problems.

One roommate—I never did find out who—had a terrible habit of leaving her birth-control patch stuck to the shower wall. No one ever admitted to the deed, but addressing it in the meetings actually made the mystery stop. Apparently the embarrassment of an open discussion was enough to make the patch bandit rethink the error of her ways. Sometimes, just addressing common issues can help put an end to them. The meeting was such a success that we held similar ones on a regular basis all year to keep us all on track. I'd highly suggest that you follow a similar strategy with your roommates.

Funny, though, we quickly learned that trash was the least of our problems.

MESS = STRESS

For me, exam time equals major stress. I tend to look for anything and everything else to do before I sit down to study. I need complete silence to concentrate, and if there is any clutter around me, I can't focus. In fact, I use the clutter as an excuse not to study, and it's usually my own piles of clothes and dirty dishes that need to be picked up before I hit the books.

Poor organizational skills really affect my study sessions. When I was in high school and couldn't find my notebooks, books, pens, and paper, I could enlist my mom's help. She stayed on my back about being organized, and if I didn't do it, she usually did. Probably not a good thing because once I arrived at college, it was up to me to find my way and learn a whole new set of skills that I didn't have at the time. My first semester was rough. From the new dorm to new friends to new classes, I was a mess. Literally. The stress of all the change finally made me realize that *I* needed to change, too. With my roommate's help, the two of us became more organized together. Simple things like designating a spot for common items made a world of difference. Assigning a spot for my books, jacket, keys, and bag helped me start organizing the rest of my life.

If the mess in your room is unavoidable, try going to the library to study. As discussed, most dorms also have a study lounge on each floor. It will serve as a night getaway from the clutter of your room and a great place to focus on your exams.

WAYS TO ESTABLISH ORDER

Now, holding meetings does not necessarily ensure that all will go smoothly. Some people are stubborn and may not be willing to change their bad habits—like ordering pizza and leaving the box and uneaten slices on the table overnight. Ants or no ants, some people refuse to modify their behavior. Also, it can be tricky if you are living with someone you barely know, but don't let this make you give up. If cleanliness is important to you, let them know, but do so without nagging them. No one wants to feel like they're being parented by one of their peers. I've had roommates in the past that ambushed me with cleaning "rules." This approach will surely add to the already-existing tension in your 10 x 12-foot dorm room. Rather than jumping on your roommates, try being polite to start the communication process.

A way to avoid the appearance of nagging is to try to compromise with a sloppy roommate. Don't like the way your roommate leaves her shoes laying around the room? Set up a space for *both of you* to put your stuff away. That way, your roommate won't feel as though she is being told what to do, but that you're both working together to keep things in order.

Take advantage of the relationship that you've built, and appreciate the fact that you know your roommate on a different level than most people do. Don't put a strain on this unique relationship because of something silly like a pile of clothes on the ground.

If you, your roommate, and your RA can't find a solution for how to live with one another, it may be time to request a new roommate.

ROOMMATES THAT REFUSE TO MEND THEIR MESSY WAYS

I'm notorious for complaining about other people's bad habits and not noticing that I, too, am guilty of the same thing. Before flying off the handle about your roommate's messy tendencies, take a deep breath and look at your own side of the room. Make sure that you are respectful of your roommate's space before you start complaining about her mess.

If all else fails, never be afraid to turn to your Resident Assistant (RA) for help. They are trained to deal with the common and uncommon issues that arise between roommates. If you, your roommate, *and* your RA can't find a solution for how to live with one another, it may be time to request a new roommate.

That's not to say that every roommate experience will work itself out. Friends of mine have had roommates that did drugs in the room, and some even stole from them. These things are not acceptable. It's up to you to know when you've reached your limit. There is always a solution, and if need be, don't be afraid to ask for a new roomie. RAs are used to these kinds of issues, and most are happy to help you find a roommate that better suits you.

When I was a freshman in college, my boyfriend went to another school, so when he came to visit, he was *always* in my room. Not only was it cramped and crowded for the two of us, but also for my poor roommate. She didn't exactly want a sleep-in guest all weekend long. It's a huge adjustment, and it's really important to be aware of not only your own needs as well as your guy's, but also how your roommate feels about having your guy around all the time. And if your roommate is unhappy with the situation, you need to ask your boy to leave soon.

THE OPPOSITE SEX

Try not to be the girlfriend that is always around—no one likes that girl. Give your guy some space, and ask that he do the same for you. Don't leave your junk lying around his room, and if he's being messy in your room, talk about it and work through it together. Communicate, communicate, communicate! If necessary, your or his RA can regulate how many nights people are staying over and put a stop to anything that is making you uncomfortable.

MAKING IT WORK

When a bunch of different personalities are thrown into one small living space, friends or *not*, people are bound to butt heads. Take responsibility for your own actions and belongings. If something's bothering you, talk about it. It's important to remember that you're living in a shared space, and rules that existed at home don't always follow you to college. But if you respect one another, your roommate situation will be a success.

making the move off campus

Anna Prestek, University of Washington–Seattle

*Y*ou may reach a point in your college career where you want to explore ditching the dorms and moving off campus. Many students do this as a way to solve the problem of warring roommates, being stuck with a party animal, or just wanting more personal space.

Considering an off-campus move but can't decide? Try making a list of the pros and cons to moving off campus to help guide the decision. Here is a list that I came up with to help get you started.

PROS

- You have complete control over your own space to arrange and decorate as you see fit. And it's always nice to have your own personal space, so you don't have to hide behind a closet door so your dorm-mate doesn't see you change.

- You have the opportunity to establish a rental history—valuable when you apply for other apartments down the road.

- It's not the most responsible reason, but once you're off campus you can throw parties without worrying about Resident Assistants breaking them up.

- Because you're the one cooking the food, it's likely a million times better than what's being served in the dining hall.

- There's something to be said for a bathroom where you don't have to wait in line for the shower and the outlets don't short out because 16 girls are trying to blow-dry their hair at the same time.

- Student apartments are usually pretty reasonable price-wise. I paid a mere $550 per month for a decent-sized room (it's probably a bit more expensive these days) that had its own bathroom, a covered parking space, and all utilities included. Yes, the apartment had lime green shag carpeting that was probably originally installed when Nixon was in office, but it was so worth it to have my own space when it came to studying and sleeping.

CONS

- Unlike in the dorm, you no longer have a built-in network of friends. You're lucky if you even see your neighbors, let alone meet them. This was something I had to deal with as an apartment-dweller; it seemed lonely without the constant flow of people coming in and out.

- You now have to deal with apartment management. Mine was a strange, senile man who would come into our apartment with no advance notice and ask, "Do you live here?" as if he had forgotten we had ever moved in. Some apartment managers seem to go out of their way to take advantage of inexperienced college student renters. Take what happened to us: our manager "lost" the list where we noted all the preexisting damages upon moving in, and my roommates and I had to pay for things that were broken long before we got there. Word to the wise: always, always make a copy of any document between you and the management and always send correspondence regarding legal matters, such as giving notice of moving out, via certified mail. Having a documented paper trail will save you from a lot of potential headaches in case something gets "lost."

- Those meals you cook? You also have to clean them up. Including the kitchen. And the bathroom. And the living room. Tasks that were once performed by a janitorial service, such as taking out the trash, are now yours. Although to a lesser degree, you still have to deal with roommates and their annoying quirks. Maybe someone doesn't take their turn doing the dishes or shortchanges you on a utility payment; whatever it is, there may still be problems with your roommate, they'll just be different problems.

- If you throw parties, the dorm staff won't break them up—but the police will.

SO YOU'VE DECIDED TO MAKE THE MOVE

If you've already decided to head off campus, now it's time to get serious about looking for your new home. The best places to look for an apartment are classifieds in student newspapers, Craigslist (www.craigslist.org), and word of mouth. Walk around the neighborhood you want to live in and look for vacancy signs. Check out a few places with your potential apartment-mates and make sure everyone agrees on a place before signing anything. Take pictures of each potential unit to compare later; after looking at, say, five units, it will be difficult to distinguish one from another. Talk to parents who have been down this road and friends who are already renting to make sure you know what to look for before you sign on the dotted line. Is it a year's lease or month-to-month? Is the damage deposit refundable? When is the rent due and where is it due? Just make sure you read everything before signing the lease and if you're unsure, ask if you can read it over and then fax or mail back after signing.

Whether you decide to stay in the dorms until graduation or leave after your first cafeteria meal, you will encounter situations there that will make you wheeze with laughter, roll your eyes in frustration, or thank the Almighty that it didn't happen in *your* room. If you move off campus you do have to take on more responsibility, but you also gain a better understanding of what it takes to make it in the post-collegiate world. And no matter where you live in college, you're in for a once-in-a-lifetime experience!

U Chic Essentials—Sharing Space

A fabulous dorm design

Your dorm room—a place where you'll be spending lots of time— should reflect who you are as a person. Love music? Try a rock icon motif. A future Anna Wintour? Deck your walls with vintage *Vogue* covers. Don't be afraid to truly express yourself in your surroundings no matter how girlie you want or do not want to go.

Accessorize it!

We all know how that right accessory can make an outfit perfect. The same goes for your dorm room. It's the special touches like some bright-colored window treatment or a funky lampshade that can really make a space your own.

Speak up

Good relationships with your roommates can go a long way in making dorm living tolerable. If things aren't going well, don't be afraid to speak up. And also be open to listening to any grievances that a roommate may have. Most problems can be resolved if both parties are willing to listen and work together.

Looking for more great advice? Head to www.UniversityChic.com and look for "U Chic Picks!" for our fav resources and websites—they come highly recommended from our guide's contributors and editors. Be sure to leave your suggestions as well!

CHAPTER 3

Head of the Class

Valedictorian in high school? Honor roll every semester? Maybe neither of these things were you. But guess what: even if you weren't at the head of your class in high school, you can still be a star in college. As any academic advisor will tell you, your high school performance does not determine your potential success in college because college is the time to pursue the things that you are good at. Bottom line: getting to the head of the class is something that everyone can do in college. The secret is that you just have to want it bad enough.

Now, before we dive into the secrets of success in school, we need to set the record straight: getting an A is not everything. It doesn't hurt, of course, but sometimes what you do outside of class matters just as much as what you do in it. Striving to do your best in school while maintaining balance with an active social and extracurricular life will help you succeed in both college and in life. So where to start in the quest to be at the head of the class? Start by reading this chapter!

which major is for me?

Kathryn Lewis, University of North Carolina—Chapel Hill

*D*o you remember those multiple-choice tests that were supposed to tell you what you should be when you grew up? I wish that choosing a major in college was as simple as filling in a few circles and waiting for a machine to do the deciding for you.

The first thing to understand and accept about choosing a major is that your first choice may backfire on you and, more important, not to be discouraged if it does. Sometimes, you find that a certain major is too hard, or too easy, or just isn't what you want to do anymore. And that's OK: it's better that you switch than study (and get an expensive degree in!) something that makes you miserable. Maybe you are afraid of an extra semester or two in school. While you should keep the costs of an extra year of school in mind, think of it this way: what is more important, graduating in four years or getting yourself set up for a job that you love? I have plenty of friends who came into college with a specific path in mind, but ended up changing after finding their true calling. College offers a lot of ideas and courses, and what you fall in love with may be something you hadn't even heard of in high school.

WHEN TO DECIDE

If you're on a strict four-year college timeline, you should not wait longer than spring semester of sophomore year to decide on your major. It is very likely that your school will have an application process and deadline (generally spring semester of sophomore year) to meet in order to be accepted into the program, and you'll likely need as much time as possible to take all the required classes for the major. An added benefit of selecting your major your sophomore year is that you have more time to meet with an advisor or counselor in that major and discuss classes and careers.

U Chic Tip!

Once you've met with your advisor, don't forget to consult the course guide each semester. It is easier than you think to forget to take that one random class required for graduation.

What if you waited until your junior year? Although it will require more effort, you still can complete your major in four years. To see just how much effort it will take, you will need to sit down soon with an advisor in your new major. If you find out during the meeting that you cannot finish the major in the next two school years, you should look into taking summer classes. In almost every case, you only have to pay per each class that you take, and it may end up being cheaper in the long run than an extra semester or two of school. And be sure to look for other ways to complete your major on time. Some colleges have a "speedy" summer session after your fourth year. At my school, UNC–Chapel Hill, this summer session is affectionately known as "Maymester." You can still walk at graduation, but you have to finish the summer classes in order to get your official diploma.

HOW DO YOU FIND A MAJOR?

The answer to this question depends entirely on your situation.

For freshmen, I can share some general advice based on my own experiences as a student. Most college students will have general education requirements. It may seem like an unimaginative and controlled system, but there are great benefits: you'll get a taste of everything, allowing you to discover a subject and potential career you might never have considered. So, for those of you who don't know what major to pursue, go for a well-rounded educational experience the first semester of your freshman year while simultaneously getting some of these requirements out of the way. Try taking intriguing classes in each area you're interested in—and some you're not!—and you may end up finding your true passion just by chance.

For non-freshmen, start by printing out a list of all of the classes that you have taken thus far. Go through the list and cross off the names of classes that made you want to scream. Next, look to see if you can spot any trends in your course selection. If you find that you mostly enjoyed your English classes, maybe you should consider a major in English. What about science? This is a pretty broad category, so you'll have to narrow the choices down. So take some more science classes! Another approach to picking a major for non-freshmen is to peruse the entire list of degrees that your school offers. There may be a major that is perfect for you that you didn't know existed. For example, I had a friend who loved her English classes and her foreign language class. And voila! With a little extra effort in looking into her options, she discovered that she could use both of these skills if she majored in Comparative Literature.

Whether you're a freshman or not, after choosing a major, you should immediately meet with an advisor or counselor that the school provides. They will help you figure out what classes you have left to take, and they will give you a general course timeline to help you graduate on time. It is always good to continually check with an advisor before signing up for classes each semester to check on your progress. Some schools may have specific advisors assigned to you while others may have certain advisors for specific majors. And don't be afraid to pick your own advisor. You may have really clicked with one professor that may end up being the best advisor you could have ever asked for, regardless of their specialty. The better the advisor knows you, the better they can assist you with making the right academic decisions and even help guide you toward scholarships, fellowships, and training that can enhance your overall education.

YOU KNOW WHAT YOU WANT TO BE, BUT NOT WHAT TO STUDY

If you come into college with a specific career in mind and you are unsure what to major in, talk to people who are working in that particular field. See what they studied in college and get advice on how they landed your future dream job. Most people are more than happy to answer questions about "how they got there," especially when you tell them that you hope to pursue a similar career path. Some schools have online databases of alumni networks that are available for student use. Don't be shy. Get in touch with these alums—and find out how they did it.

After you make a connection, keep up with them throughout school and even after your college years. These individuals can become mentors who will help guide you along your career path. Keep them updated on your progress and be sure to write thank-you notes. And don't forget: one important key to getting jobs after college is connections. Knowing someone in the field who is aware of your work ethic and commitment (and who is from your school) can be incredibly helpful. So, make an effort to stay in touch.

Most people are more than happy to answer questions about "how they got there," especially when you tell them that you hope to pursue a similar career path.

WARNING! YOU MAY HAVE PICKED THE WRONG MAJOR

If you are getting bad grades in classes and you are not feeling motivated to do the work, you may be going down the wrong path. If your GPA is below 2.0 for a semester and you put in an honest effort, it could be an indication that you're pursuing the wrong major. (If it's something else, like too much drinking and partying, be honest with yourself about it.) You should not have to struggle just to get through the major that is right for you. I am not saying that every class is going to be wonderful and completely stress-free, but you should feel like it is worth the effort that you're putting into it.

CHANGING YOUR MAJOR

If you discover halfway through college that you were not meant to be a chemical engineering major, for example, get out fast. But be sure to call your parents or whoever is helping fund your education to loop them in on the decision and to logically explain why you have to switch majors. Explain that it would be a total waste of your abilities to stick with a course of studies that is making you cry every night and that you're likely to fail. Your parents will (probably) understand, because in the end, they want you to be happy.

Once you have decided to change your major and have made the necessary phone calls, you need to make an appointment with an advisor. Some of you may even have to go to the advisor within your current major to get their approval to change. Get started as soon as possible. You are initially going to have a lot of paperwork to change your major, but just remember why it's so important to you and that you'll soon be studying a subject you love.

GOING FOR A MINOR

If there is an additional area of study that you find yourself interested in but don't have the time to pursue as a major, why not go for a minor? I'm studying graphic design, but I also enjoy writing, so I've decided to minor in creative writing. Why did I go for it? I was writing so much in my free time that I thought, "Why not get credit for it?"

It is also possible that if you've taken lots of classes in a specific area (i.e., if you changed majors halfway through), you may end up with enough credits or close to enough credits to minor in that topic. My older brother was surprised to find out his senior year that he had enough credits to minor in history if he took one more class. No surprise, he decided to go for it. Having a minor shows ambition and well-roundedness to future employers or grad schools, and it can add fun and variety to your education.

THE END GOAL

Would you rather have a career that you love or finish school on time? Yes, doing both would be ideal, but sometimes that's just not realistic. The real reason you go to college is to help you discover your life's path—but this doesn't happen overnight. In fact, on average, it usually takes a college student more than four years to graduate. So don't be afraid if you are going to have to stay a little bit longer to pursue a course of study that you are totally passionate about. Choosing a major is not easy, but once you have figured it out, you've already made a "major" accomplishment in discovering your path to success in college and in life.

how to get to the top

Jennifer Rubino, Kean University

There are many different ways to get top grades. For one, you could literally sit at the head of the class—in the front of the classroom. This actually works for many reasons. You're forced to pay more attention to the professor, you'll always have an unobstructed view, and there is no one to hide behind during class discussions.

But sitting in the front row will not guarantee you top grades: there's no way to avoid the work and responsibility that comes along with being a top student these days. Hard work is the only way to get ahead. Lucky for me, my high school prepared me well. I was ready to buckle down as a college student after facing the challenges of high school and going through the college application process. But it was not just my high school preparation that put me at the top. I also had a strategy to be successful from the start. Want to get to the head of the class? Read on to find out how.

THE STRATEGY

When you're going for top honors, let's be honest—it's competitive. Would you head into a sporting competition without a success strategy? That is why I highly recommend devoting some time to developing a plan for your study and achievement. With a little effort, this strategy will help you, at a minimum, keep up with the competition. At its best, you'll be at the top.

THE GOOD, THE BAD, AND THE UGLY

After you've attended all your courses the first week of the semester (btw, this advice applies to all semesters going forward—going to class is the best way to make sure you pass), take a couple of hours over the weekend to devise your "strategy" for the semester. Try to determine which courses seem like they'll be fairly easy for you or won't require too much work and which ones could end up being a nightmare. Some things to look out for in separating the tough from the easy courses: the existence or frequency of quizzes, number of required papers, midterms, term papers, and yes, the final. If a particular course has more of these items than not, you're most likely dealing with a class that's going to keep you really busy.

Once you've categorized your classes, figure out a schedule that will have you spending the right amount of time on each course in order to keep up with all of the readings and assignments without completely stressing yourself out. Also, be ready to revise this strategy along the way if necessary. With a good schedule, you will not be surprised by any pop quizzes, you will stay on track for any midterm or term papers, and finals preparation will be a whole lot easier than if you waited until the last minute to catch up.

IF ANYTHING, JUST GO

Attendance is a major factor in being successful in school. Students who attend class often are far more likely to succeed than students who do not attend class. Any professor who you speak with will back this up. At some point you'll probably hear something along these lines: "Ninety percent of success is showing up," because for a lot of students the hard part is getting to class. If you have to be absent from a class, pair up with someone who is also in it. This way, there is someone to contact about what was assigned and discussed that day and even to get notes from. Also, make up any missed work as soon as possible. Being absent is an easy way to fall behind and lose a spot at the head of the class. From my own experience, showing up on time and being ready to learn is the only real way to get ahead.

PAY ATTENTION TO YOUR COMMUNICATION STYLE

While your communication style is hugely important in your social life, it also has a specific role in getting good grades. Sure, tests and quizzes also have a significant role in getting that coveted A on the report card, but take a look at your syllabus that covers the grading scale in your classes and you'll often find that a percentage of your grade is tied to that elusive "classroom participation" factor.

So what does this mean for your strategy? For anyone who aspires to be at the top, you first have to understand your communication preferences. Ask yourself, "Am I a good listener who is somewhat shy in a public setting, or am I someone who enjoys speaking up and debating from time to time on subjects that interest me?" Understanding your personal preferences for classroom involvement is key to figuring out how to stand out in the classroom regardless of whether you're shy or on the chatty side. If you're shy, make an effort to speak at least once a week on a subject that you either know a lot about or are somewhat passionate about. The knowledge or passion will help carry you through your shyness. Also, take time to go visit your professor during office hours so that he or she can get to know who you are and come to appreciate your efforts even if you're not speaking up on a daily basis. And if you're the gregarious type, by all means, speak up! However, you need to be careful that you're not speaking simply in order to hear your own voice. Your classmates and professor will know the distinction. Make sure that your comments are thoughtful and either advance the discussion or introduce a new idea. By planning your strategy for communication inside the classroom, you're guaranteeing that you're meeting your professor's expectations for A-worthy classroom participation.

VOLUNTEER

We all know that community service is an important component of being a college student. Guess what? Volunteering in class can also help you get ahead. When the professor asks for someone to volunteer for *anything*, be the first to take the assignment. Taking the initiative is a great tool for success. I had a professor in college that gave extra credit to anyone who volunteered to do something for the class.

WHAT YOU CAN DO OUTSIDE OF CLASS

Now that you've got a strategy for success, it's time to focus on how you'll conduct yourself outside of the class in order to ensure your success.

Make a study schedule—and stick to it

Besides attending class, a few hours per week must be dedicated to homework and studying. There is just no way around it. Most likely, quizzes and exams will make up the majority of a class grade, so good study skills are crucial to graduating at the top of the class. A few nights before the test or quiz, reread any notes and material that will be covered. It may also be a good idea to write a summary of the notes that were taken in class. From my experience, it takes an average of one to two hours of studying per week for each class to get a good grade (although this varies with different majors). This advice, however, does not apply to midterms and finals. These items are special and are discussed further below.

Find your favorite study place

For most people, the best place to study is a quiet environment that will have zero distractions. Instead of your dorm room, where you can easily slack off to take a nap or surf the Web, opt for the library or a designated study area on campus. If you're more extroverted and get more done with people around you, a coffeehouse can be a good place to hit the books—especially since you'll have quick access to caffeine to keep you going. It's OK (in fact encouraged!) to treat yourself to a snack while studying. It will give you more energy, and is an incentive to get through the material.

> It's OK (in fact encouraged!) to treat yourself to a snack while studying. It will give you more energy, and is an incentive to get through the material.

Form a study group

This tip doesn't work for everyone. Some of us are more social, and others prefer a more isolated environment. But if you like studying with other people, it can be useful to have them to interact with. For example, you can ask for their help if you're having difficulty with the material. Also, you might feel more inspired to study if your fellow students are in the trenches with you, and you can help each other stay motivated. I was never part of a study group. I get distracted too easily by other people, especially if there happens to be someone attractive in the group! I find that the more people involved, the more likely studying will turn into socializing. However, if you can find a group of people who share your dedication to staying on task, it can be a great experience.

Treat yourself right

Good preparation for class involves allowing yourself a good night's sleep, getting regular exercise, and making an effort to eat healthy. These activities are proven to help classroom performance. Exercise is also of great importance. There are tons of scientific studies showing how good exercise is for your brain. I suggest reading some of them if you ever need some motivation to go to the gym! While weightlifting and walking are good, it is generally thought that vigorous cardiovascular exercise (30 minutes or more of running or biking, for example) is the best workout for your mind.

Success can be dependent on what you eat

And finally, a couple key points on eating healthy. Breakfast is the most important meal of the day! It sets your mood and energy level every morning for the whole day. Stay away from the sugary coffee drinks—if you need them, at least save them for an afternoon break. Try not to become a caffeine addict—save it for when you need it. If you are a Starbucks fiend, consider that a regular tall coffee (12 oz.) has almost 6 times as much caffeine as a 12-oz. Diet Coke. If you love your caffeine, at least have it in moderation.

Start the day with anything that has a decent amount of protein
in it, because protein decreases your hunger better than carbs and
provides a steady energy source all morning. Eggs, nuts, health
bars, and many other foods are perfect for this. Just find what you
like and make sure it has some protein.

Fat also provides a steady energy source and decreases your
appetite more than carbs do; just don't overdo the trans fats
and saturated fats that are in donuts, creams, and the like. Also
remember that with too many carbs, you will get an energy high
and crash a couple hours later, which is no good for learning. If
you still need your bread or bagel, try to make it wheat or whole
grain, which will help keep your energy level more even over a
longer period of time.

AFTER-HOURS

No, I'm not talking about partying here (but of course you should
have fun too!). A student does not need to be failing to want to
improve a grade. Extra help is available for anyone who simply
wants to do better. There are usually tutors or study sessions on
campus. This could add an additional hour or two on top of what

you're already doing outside of class, but it will be well spent.

Also, make an effort to get to know your professors. They like to see that their students are interested in their class. Make time to talk to a professor about their material. Discuss anything of interest and ask them any questions about the subject. If your effort was sincere, they will most likely take this into consideration when it comes time to give you a final grade.

STAY ORGANIZED

Every semester you receive so many handouts and take so many notes for each class that it can be hard to keep track of all of them. Many of my teachers recommended a three-ring binder that is categorized by date and subject. This way, notes can be easily located when it comes to preparing for a test or quiz. Students who are disorganized waste time looking for notes instead of preparing for the exam itself. I also use highlighters to keep track of any important information. Note cards and Post-its can also be useful.

Another way to keep organized is to keep an assignment book. List each assignment's due date and make sure to refer to it every day. Then, check off each assignment as it is completed; it's a great way to make sure everything gets done on time. Make sure to prioritize since the workload can get heavy at times.

TRY STAYING AHEAD OF THE GAME

Completing assignments a few days before they are due is a good idea. It allows you extra time to make any last-minute changes or revisions in the work before it's graded. In general, make sure you are consistently knowledgeable about the coursework as the semester progresses rather than cramming the day before a test, midterm, or final. By staying on top of things, you will save time (and your sanity!) when it comes to studying for a difficult exam, midterm, or final since there won't be as much to review.

REGISTER FOR COURSES ASAP!

Another thing to do ahead of time is register for classes as soon as possible. Be sure to pick up a catalog as soon as you can, even before you get to school, and browse through the classes to see which seem the most interesting. You will find that the good courses (those that are either easy or have fantastic professors) fill up quickly—as do the courses that everyone in your major needs to graduate.

Even if it means waking up early to get in line and register for those classes, it's completely worth losing a few extra hours of sleep. It's a lot easier to get ahead when classes are genuinely interesting and enjoyable. Also take note of any professors that were recommended by your friends. People who have taken the class before definitely have the inside scoop. To see what students on your campus are saying about a particular course or professor at your school, visit websites like RateMyProfessor.com or PickAProf. com. Each site collects ratings from hundreds of students at your school and provides you instant access to this data. And don't forget that you can also rate your previous professors and courses while you're there.

ACTUALLY DO THE READING

Reading is another way to get ahead and be more knowledgeable about a subject. By actually reading your textbooks and other materials, you'll gain a deeper understanding of the subject. Many students do not want to dedicate the time to read or even purchase their college textbooks, but it's foolish to try and rely solely on a professor's notes and lectures. Reading books is the only way to be fully prepared for class, since the professor assigns those books for specific reasons. And it is impossible for the professor to discuss everything that will be covered on the tests or quizzes. Therefore it is your responsibility to read everything you are assigned when it's assigned and be ready to discuss it or take a quiz on it.

MIDTERMS AND FINALS

Midterms and finals can seem overwhelming, especially since they usually cover a lot of information. Don't try to study the material for each course all at once or else it will be too much to remember and possibly overwhelm you. Start early and study a little bit at a time. Take it chapter by chapter and slowly begin to become familiar with the information. Only at the very end will everything be integrated. Also, one strategy that worked for me was to focus on one test at a time. If I had two tests in one week, I would study nothing else except the material for these courses. This kept my stress level down to a minimum, and I was able to go into each exam feeling very confidently prepared.

FINALLY, REPUTATION MATTERS

Work on building a reputation for being one of the most dedicated and responsible students in your class. Your professor will greatly appreciate it, and this can also serve as a deciding factor when it comes to grades.

U Chic Tip!

Many students hand things in late or ask for an extension. If you want to get ahead, don't do this. If you really are spending too much time on an assignment, it is time to ask for help. Work hard to stay on top, but if for some reason your efforts aren't paying off, talk with your professor to make sure that you understand the material. This will prevent you from falling behind and possibly even failing a course.

No one said that it's easy to be on top. As you'll find, it can take a lot of time to get ahead. But, if you follow some of the advice above, this is definitely an achievable goal. Graduating with high honors and an impressive grade point average is something you can be proud of after graduation, as well as something that will help you get ahead in the future. The hard work and determination you will need are worth it.

f.i.n.a.l.s.: fudge, I never actually learned squat!

Olga Belogolova, Boston University

ake a list. Check it twice. Maybe three times. Maybe even four. Where did the semester go? Where did those simple days of just worrying about homework go? Times have changed, and all of a sudden you find yourself cramming for that dreaded final exam.

STUDY STYLES

One of the most important steps in successfully studying for a final exam is finding out your study style. Study styles vary depending on what kind of learner you are and how well you remember important information. Another thing to take into consideration is how good of a note-taker you've been all semester and if you've been following the reading.

For the "I love to take obsessive notes/I've done all my reading" student

For those good note-takers out there, the obsessive-compulsive ones who write down everything the professors say, the challenge is narrowing things down. Grab that nice, big highlighter and your note-filled notebook and find a comfortable chair to curl up in. *It's time to power through it.* In getting started, first ask yourself, "What's on the exam?" If there's a list of terms or ideas or even chapters, make sure that, as you go through your notes, you're collating your lists and highlighting only the most important stuff. The next step depends on what you like to do. If you're one of those people who loves index cards with a passion—you know, one of those people who buys index cards in different colors, shapes, sizes, and maybe even with a spiral going through them—grab that stack of blank note cards and write out all the highlighted terms from your notebook.

U Chic Tip!

If your laptop is with you wherever you go, like mine is, open a Word document and get cracking on retyping out the important sections of your notes—a condensed crib sheet.

Writing things down and rereading them again and again, at least three times, will immerse your mind in the key terms and ideas you need to know. And before you know it, the knowledge you will need to ace the test will just be there.

For the "I fell asleep during lecture/I prefer doodling to notes" student

For those of you who fell asleep on that severely uncomfortable wooden lecture desk or daydreamed about the boy sitting in the front row, or just forgot to write things down because you needed to finish that elaborate design on the corner of your spiral notebook, it might be a bit harder to catch up. But don't give up; it can be done.

Here's what you need to do to quickly get on track. Take whatever is left of your doodled notebook (or just get a new one), head to the library, and take the books you were supposed to read for class. Since you are short on time, there is no way you can read through all the required material in time for the exam. Not to worry. Actually, the worst thing you can do right now is to freak out.

Now that you know what might be on the exam (especially if your professor told you during a review session or handed you some sort of study guide), your catch-up reading can be *very* focused. Go through and skim the chapters that are relevant. Make sure to make good use of the table of contents and the index to focus your reading. Once you've read what you needed to and have taken some quality notes, start making a study guide.

Since you still might not be sure that you have all the notes you need, your best option is probably to opt for a study group. For a lot of people, the best way to learn is to explain concepts to your friends and classmates, and have them explained to you.

> The worst thing you can do right now
> is to freak out.

So, get your fellow classmates together—they'll likely come willingly, as they're already studying for the test, too. A good group session in the student union or outside (depending on the weather) is a perfect way to get a lot of work done in the precious few days (or even hours!) that you have to catch up before the exam.

> For a lot of people, the best way to
> learn is to explain concepts to your
> friends and classmates.

IT'S OK TO TAKE A BREAK

A good study session involves some necessary breaks. Breaks can involve food, drink, and sometimes even a little fun. Sometimes the best study break is taking a moment, stepping away from the books and the computer, and blasting your favorite dancing tune of the week. It's like having a mini dance party. Close your eyes, dance your little heart away, and then get back to work. Jumping jacks also work.

When it comes to food, make sure to have a balance of healthy snacks and complete crap food. Proteins and healthy fats are a good way to start a long study session (a peanut butter sandwich on wheat bread is simple and healthy), but it's OK to throw in an apple or banana when you need that extra burst of energy.

When it comes to drinks, I know coffee is certainly a tempting option and so is that can of Monster or Red Bull staring down at you from your bookshelf. Resist. When it comes to coffee— and I am sure you've heard it a million times—the higher you climb, the harder you fall. It might give you that initial boost, but when you are trying to stay awake during your exam and the floor starts spinning, those cups of coffee won't seem like such a great idea anymore.

The best and most often underestimated option is actually water. Buy a massive bottle of water or two and just keep drinking it. If the liquid keeps going through your system, it will revitalize and keep you awake without the negative or counterproductive effects of caffeine or taurine, the stuff that gives you wings but turns you into a monster later.

SETTING GOALS

Reward yourself for a job well done—or just done. When I was a kid, my mom used to make me do my math homework at the kitchen table. Lucky for me, she is a math teacher. She used to make me a nice snack or put a chocolate bar in front of me and she would say, "*Olya* (my Russian name), *finish this page of math problems and then you can reward yourself.*"

I hated it. So when she walked out of the room, I would sneak a bite. Why should I wait? I used to hate having to miss swim practice because I was not done with my homework or because my room wasn't clean. Why did I have to finish it first? Why couldn't I just go to practice and then finish my work when I got home?

As I grew older, however, I learned the value of these lessons and have turned them into a sort of self-discipline. Granted, there is a good deal of procrastination that goes into that equation, but I am less inclined to procrastinate when I know that I can go out to that party on Saturday night only if I have my final study guide ready. Also, let's face it: Facebook stalking and messaging friends on AIM is not as appealing as the reward at the end of the road.

Just tell yourself, if I finish reading through 4 chapters tonight, I can go meet my friend for coffee tomorrow. This way, you get part of your work done and you also get to take a well-deserved break.

FIND OUT HOW YOU STUDY

Alert, Alert! Tempting beds operating in your area! Move away from all pillows and couches immediately! Your safety depends on it…or at least your studying does.

Where you choose to study, once again, depends on what kind of studier you are. One piece of advice that I feel definitely applies to everyone is to get out of your room! Don't fall into the trap of, "Oh I'll just read my sociology book in my bed, it's so comfortable." No matter how enthralling your world history or philosophy book is, reading about fascist dictators or the Socratic method will not keep you awake if you are surrounded by the cloud of your comforter. I'm not saying you won't fall asleep at the library, but most likely the wooden desk where your head would rest is not anywhere near as cushiony, soft, or inviting. If you fall asleep, you most likely won't be there for long.

Library

Your school's library is a good place to get some studying done. Not only are you surrounded by other students who share your study woes, but you are also surrounded by bookshelves. Even if you don't feel the need to grab one of those books for some extra pre-final reading, the sheer power of all of those books should inspire you to get down and dirty with your studies. The library might not be appealing to those who prefer to be invisible during finals time because it will be filled with people, but remember they are all there for the same reason. If you want a good balance between social life and intense studies, the library always works.

U Chic Tip!

How to make the library work? First, some libraries have more social floors and areas that you can seek out when you head over with your laptop bag and a handy study buddy. Find a nice place to sit with your friends and once in a while stop to ask questions or maybe even chat a little. The best thing about bringing a study buddy with you is that you can pop out to take an ice cream break without having to completely pack up and get off track. You can leave your precious laptop with your trusty friend. When you're studying solo, head to the quieter floors or areas to get some serious studying done.

Loud/social areas

If you are one of those people who find silence way too quiet in a creepy kind of way, perhaps you should opt for a louder and more bustling study area. Sometimes a little background commotion is all you need to actually get some work done. If you're one of those people who can't handle the silence of the library or your own room, head to a coffee shop or maybe even a student union hangout. There will be tons of people around and you can opt for some breaks while you are there without having to move an inch. Other benefits of this option are that you can eat while you work. Just one piece of advice: make sure you remember to take down that Abercrombie model wallpaper you have set as your desktop background. No one wants to see it. Or maybe they do, but either way, I speak from experience when I tell you to put up a pretty picture of a beach somewhere. You never know who will walk by your computer while you're studying at the downtown coffee shop.

Studying with others

Be forewarned: study buddies are not for everyone. A study buddy or even a study group can be a great thing for you, but it can also be distracting or disastrous depending on the type of person you are. Usually, a study buddy is a friend with whom you can get work done. He or she doesn't necessarily have to be in your class or even in your major, just someone you know you can be quiet with and bounce ideas off of as needed.

Study buddies can be great, but make sure you are ready to take on the distraction and avoid the pitfalls of chatting instead of getting some studying done. Bottom line: embrace the distraction that a study buddy might bring, but don't overuse it. Make sure that both of you do some studying and help each other with anything you can.

If for some reason, you feel the need to go home or somewhere else to work on your own, don't feel obligated to stay with your friend. Finals are a stressful time and good friends understand. Studying together is not primarily a social activity, so they should not be offended if you have to leave for some quiet time.

Study groups

Study groups tend to be a little more focused than a couple of study buddies sitting around together. Usually study groups involve people from your class and not necessarily close friends. This is great because you can delegate and divide up the studying work and share it with one another, teaching and learning at the same time without the major temptation to dish on the hottest gossip. Make a list of all the topics you need to know and get ready to divvy up the work. Everyone in the group should have some work to do and report back to everyone else—you can even make a group study guide out of the combined work and give a copy to each person. If you plan to work in a study group for finals, be sure to start way before finals so each group member gets a chance to review everything, and not just their part of the study guide.

Dealing with the stress

If finals are around the corner, be prepared to accept the fact that it is going to be stressful. There's nothing that you can do about it besides accepting it and moving on; the worst thing you can do is stress about being stressed out.

There are many ways of dealing with finals stress, but some are better than others. The main idea is to take plenty of breaks. Try going to the gym or take the edge off with a swim. Really, any form of physical activity should do the trick. Don't think that exercise will make you tired and leave you too worn out to work. In fact, exercise does just the opposite. It releases endorphins that make you feel better and helps you be even more focused when you sit back down in front of your books.

> The worst thing you can do is stress about being stressed out.

As for other stress-relieving activities, some schools organize fun events during finals that help chase the stress bug away. Last winter, my friend Hillary and I went to an on-campus event for stressed students in the student union. It was a great idea. Students were getting free massages, taking breaks to play ping-pong with their friends, and much more. Keep your eyes open for similar opportunities on your campus. And if they're not there, seek off-campus ways to pamper yourself during finals, like getting a facial or manicure. The most important thing to remember when dealing with stress is that working too hard or too much might not always be the best strategy for getting a good score on your final exam. Sometimes, all you need is a break or good night's sleep to let all of your hard work sink in. After all, there is only so much you can do.

And the rest? It's up to karma, or something like that.

U Chic Essentials—Head of the Class

Don't be shy
Never be shy about asking others, especially alumni and professors, for advice. Besides getting great advice on what major to pursue, how to do better in class, or which internship to go for, alums want to help. Bottom line: it's never too early to start networking with this all-important group of people.

Always think two steps ahead
Love the classes you're currently taking in humanities? Consider how you can turn this love into a career. By thinking two steps ahead, you will be that much closer to figuring out what you were *born to do* after college.

Team up
One surefire way to get to the head of the class is to team up. Join a study group or find a study buddy. Depending on your learning style, either option will pay multiple dividends by keeping you on track, ensuring that the material makes sense, and pitching in whenever you're unable to attend. Success guaranteed.

Looking for more great advice? Head to www.UniversityChic.com and look for "U Chic Picks!" for our fav resources and websites—they come highly recommended from our guide's contributors and editors. Be sure to leave your suggestions as well!

CHAPTER 4

Getting Involved

The previous chapter focused on getting to the head of the class. Well, this chapter is about forgetting everything that was said in the previous chapter and focusing on how to have a life *outside of class*. Just kidding—don't forget *everything*! We just felt it was important to address your extracurricular life, which is equally important to your studies.

When it comes to getting involved in college, just follow your instinct. Find your niche—that special thing that you will do in college—and start it as soon as possible. By carving out time for that niche early on, you're ensuring that this will be a priority throughout your collegiate life, so when the going gets tough (like during finals), you know that you can always come back to your fav activities when the stress dies down. Also, by getting involved in extracurriculars early on, you're giving yourself additional opportunities to expand your horizons, possibly leading to great things like internships and even jobs as you get closer to graduation. Not to mention all the friends you'll make!

One word of caution: watch out for the "buffet effect." With everything that you have to choose from, you may have an urge to try everything and overindulge, so to speak. Don't. Getting involved in too many things can take you away from the main reason that you are in college in the first place—to get a great education. So get involved, but make sure not to put too much on your plate. Read on for some great insights on your life *outside of the classroom*!

ditch the dorm, get a life!

Anna Prestek, University of Washington—Seattle

*D*uring your tenure as a dorm dweller, you will be presented with myriad opportunities to socialize with others on your floor at parties, dances, movies, and outings. All these activities are fun, a great way to meet the other people you live with, and a perfect opportunity to relax after a busy week filled with tests and papers. Taking time to have fun is an extremely necessary part of school because, let's face it, you will burn out *way* before you complete your four or five years in higher education if you don't take time to just chill. Having said that, another vital and rewarding aspect of college life extends beyond the confines of the dormitory—get involved with something, either on campus or beyond.

Picking Up Stories and Guys

Johannah Cornblatt, Harvard University

When I walked into the newsroom of the *Harvard Crimson* the first day of my freshman year, I noticed instructions on how to open a document for a new story taped prominently on the wall. But after I saw a cute sophomore boy sitting at the desk across from mine, I pretended not to see the directions and, sweetly, solicited his help. It was like that scene in *Mean Girls* when Cady claims to be bad at math in order to convince Aaron, the charming senior, to tutor her. I didn't play dumb for long, though. News editors quickly sent me to interview students around campus for a story on e-registration, a new feature (pretty standard these days) that allowed us to sign up for classes online. Halfway through writing my article back in the newsroom, I glanced up at the clock and realized I had missed dinner. Luckily, aforementioned cute sophomore had also lost track of the time. He asked me out to a burrito place across the street, and so began my years-long romance with my college boyfriend—and, that same night, my relationship with Harvard's daily newspaper. I'm definitely not the only *Crimson* editor guilty of what they call "Crimcest." You'd be amazed how good even the nerdiest Harvard boy looks when you're stuck laying out the paper together at 4 a.m.

While the *Crimson* can certainly spice up your love life, another big perk of working on the newspaper for me was the friends. I met two of my current roommates at the *Crimson* during the first week of our freshman year, and we've spent many a late night together in the newsroom since. One is now an executive editor like me, and the other, who writes a biweekly column, is now Harvard's Ann Coulter (although she notes that she's "not insane or anti-Semitic, only conservative and blonde"). I remember how the three of us idolized the senior girls on the *Crimson* when we were freshmen, and it's funny seeing younger girls look up to us like that now. Friendships really cross class years at organizations like the *Crimson*, and girls who have graduated still keep in touch with us, offering advice on everything from boys to careers.

Whether it's for your own pleasure or to enhance your résumé, making an effort to venture beyond the dorm can enhance both your outlook on life and your curriculum vitae. Figuring out how to get involved in a student organization can seem daunting at first. Fear not: there are many tips and tricks to help you negotiate your way into having a fulfilling life outside of class. Branching out beyond the dorm will expose you to new people and activities.

WHERE TO START

When you're first exploring your options in the extracurricular field, think of what interests you. Is it playing a particular sport? Speaking a foreign language? Film noir? Bible study? Whatever it is, chances are there is a club in honor of it on your college campus. And if there isn't, you can always start one yourself. Because there are so many options in college, the difficulty will be in narrowing down the playing field to activities that really interest you.

If you need some help brainstorming what clubs might catch your fancy, here are a few ideas to get you started:

Are grades your thing?

Does the thought of spending more time studying to achieve that latest A or honor make shivers of joy run down your spine? If this is you, consider applying to an on-campus honor society. Many departments have their own honor society or there can be one for an entire class such as Phi Eta Sigma, the honor society that academically inclined freshmen can join at the University of Washington (UW) after achieving a specific GPA and the required community service hours. The benefits of honor society membership are twofold: one, let's face it, they look great on a résumé. It shows that you aim high, achieve the goals you set, and are intelligent and disciplined. Second, your honor society peers are great study partners and the element of positive peer pressure can further your academic ambitions. Third, you may be required to devote time to community service in projects that are for good causes, which can get you out into the world and make you feel great about yourself.

Do you have a deep-seated desire to dive for a Frisbee while others give chase and tug at your jersey?

Or does soccer sound like the perfect way to bond with your fellow man or woman? If the answer is yes, it sounds like an intramural sports team or league is the way to go. These teams range from all-out competition where players vie for titles and trophies to weekend bowling leagues where teams compete for beers and bragging rights. You'll be able to find the level of play you're looking for, and if not, put up some fliers and start a team!

Do you dream in different languages?

Fantasize about traveling to foreign lands? Indulge your inner wanderlust without having to pony up for a pesky passport. Foreign language clubs and language exchange programs are a great way to get immersed in a new language, brush up on skills carried over from your high school French class, and even help an exchange student practice his or her English.

U Chic Tip!

Other options for clubs and organizations, both on and off campus, include:

On Campus:

- Student radio shows or newspapers
- Church groups or Bible study
- Student government
- Heritage-oriented clubs (Korean, Native American, African American, etc.)
- Photography
- Political clubs (Young Democrats, Young Republicans, etc.)

- On-campus magazines or journals
- Music groups: choir, jazz, a cappella
- Spoken word, poetry slam
- Martial arts
- Lifestyle-focused clubs: vegan, cooking, etc.
- Seasonal outdoor activities: snowboarding, wakeboarding, boating, etc.
- Theater and improv groups
- TV show viewing club
- Nature clubs: camping, bird watching, wetlands, ocean beaches
- Study-centric clubs: become a peer tutor in English, writing, math, or other subjects
- Volunteer and advocacy groups: Habitat for Humanity, Voices for Planned Parenthood, PETA, etc.
- Dance: swing, ballroom, etc.
- Mentorship clubs: meeting with upper classmen to talk and get their feedback and advice on the college experience

Off Campus:

- Volunteer as a docent at a museum or art gallery
- Serve as a mentor in a local chapter of the Boys & Girls Clubs
- Join a professional networking group based on your study area; for instance, communications or public relations majors can join the Public Relations Student Society of America (PRSSA). Many of these professional organizations require membership fees but offer lower membership rates for college students.

THE COMMITMENT

Wherever you think your passion lies, it's important to ask yourself if it's something that you are, indeed, passionate about and interested in. There are things you will tell others you are passionate about because they sound noble (volunteering to help children in Third World countries, for example), and then there are the things you truly love to do. Make sure that you don't neglect getting involved in something that goes into that "truly love to do" category. It will make you happier overall, and thus better able to succeed in and enjoy the other things you are involved in. Also, those activities you sign up for just because you truly enjoy them sometimes end up being the ones that look the best on your résumé—when you do things you are truly passionate about, you will be more willing and likely to rise to a leadership position.

The caveat is to remember to take part in something that you genuinely believe you can commit time to, even if it's just for a few hours a week. If you have a busy schedule with other commitments such as sports or work, make sure that you take these activities into consideration when getting involved. Before getting committed to anything, you need to be fully aware of the expectations for group membership and whether you can meet them before getting involved.

There are activities you will tell others you are passionate about because they sound noble (volunteering to help children in Third World

countries, for example) and there are the things
you truly love to do. Make sure that you don't
neglect getting involved in something that goes
into that "truly love to do" category.

Some groups are more dependent on attendance while others
are more laid-back. For instance, to be part of a book club, reading
the assigned book before the next meeting is required. If you didn't
do the reading, you can't be a star discussion member. So when
considering whether to take up a new activity, just make sure you
will be able to juggle the timing in your hectic collegiate schedule.
You don't want to leave anyone hanging if you're not able to make
a meeting, but you also don't want to be needlessly stressed on top
of your already busy days. Extracurricular activities are meant to be
a fun, bonding experience, not an added stressor.

PURSUING YOUR ACADEMIC INTERESTS WITH EXTRACURRICULARS

If you're at a point in your studies where you have a good idea of
what you'd like to major in, you can also check out meetings or
gatherings in different academic departments. Many departments
post their clubs and functions in student lounges and places within
the department such as study and writing centers. You can also
find out about many of these opportunities online.

Best thing about these get-togethers? You don't have to
necessarily be a "declared major" to take part. Before I declared

my major in English, I often took part in Castalia, a monthly gathering held by the English Department in which students and faculty listened to a group of selected graduate students read their latest works. Even before I was officially in the major, this was a fun way to get to know other undergrad and grad English majors while participating in a function held by the department that I was interested in joining.

U Chic Tip! Focus Your Efforts
Maggie Biunno, Hofstra University

Don't try to take on too much! This tip worked for me. When I started college, I focused on joining a few groups like the school newspaper. I started at the bottom as a staff writer, moved up to an assistant position, then feature editor, and finished as the managing editor—second in charge of the entire paper! The best part about being involved in the paper was the opportunity to use what I learned inside the classroom. Thanks to this experience, I discovered that I wanted to be more than just a writer. I wanted to be an editor as well. What could prepare me for the future better than that?

ORGANIZATIONS WITH A SIGNIFICANT TIME COMMITMENT

Groups like the school's dance team, choir, orchestra, and band require a large time commitment. These groups will not try to hide this from you. At the first meeting they should be able to tell you what kind of commitment they expect from their members. If you find yourself enjoying the organization's activities, then it should be worth your time. You just have to make sure that you are not letting your academics fall short and that you are managing your time wisely.

START YOUR OWN ORGANIZATION

If you've been looking at the opportunities on campus and you can't find an organization that you want to join, why not start your own? Just realize that starting an organization will be fairly time-consuming—you are going to have to find members and work to get the organization recognized (and funded) by the university. Chances are that if you are interested in an area and a club does not exist for it yet, it won't be that tough to find people who are looking for a similar organization.

Getting involved on campus may at first seem overwhelming. But if you have a good idea about activities on campus that might interest you and keep an eye out for opportunities, joining a club or volunteer group can greatly supplement your years at school. It's a great way to meet people that you might not meet in class or in the dorm and get exposed to activities that the dorm doesn't offer.

for the future madam president

Alexa Rozell, Georgetown University

Y ou walk onto campus for the first time, ready to make a difference. All through high school, you demonstrated leadership potential—captain of your varsity volleyball team, president of the National Honor Society, secretary of your senior class. You want to continue working with student associations in college, and more important, you want to do this as a leader. This section is for all you natural-born leaders wanting to get up-and-running as your class leader.

So where to start? I was in your position less than a year ago. I had no idea where to even begin getting involved in the student government association at my school. Well, with a little bit of effort and seeking out the right connections, I now serve as the chair of the Freshman Class Committee at Georgetown University. Thanks to this experience, I have a little advice to share that can help you access the halls of leadership on your campus.

GETTING INVOLVED IN STUDENT GOVERNMENT

In your quest to become a student government leader, you first need to decide what level of participation you want to have within the organization. Stop by the student government office on your campus to find more information on all your options.

Many campuses offer students a wide variety of student government opportunities, requiring anywhere from a little to a lot of your time. A word of caution: do not pledge yourself to a large commitment before you know what other organizations you want to join. If given the chance, student government can become a huge part of your life, and take up a lot of your free time. I regularly spend around 7 hours a week for my Freshman Class chair duties, and I see other student body leaders spending many more hours in their offices. It is an amazing experience and extremely fun, but you need to first make sure you know what kind of time commitment you are looking for before you sign on for a project or position.

Most universities offer students the opportunity to be involved in different branches of the student government, including the executive board, the senate, and spots on small committees that are dedicated to a single issue. The more public-oriented positions will require a campus-wide election. At the beginning of your first semester, you will see information on how to run for specific positions such as the senate. However, the smaller committees are generally appointed positions, especially for freshmen. If an election is required for a smaller role, it is held in the spring. Therefore, freshmen are usually appointed to these areas on an as-needed basis.

Don't be afraid to ask upperclassmen in student government at your school how they initially got involved and in what programs they would recommend that you participate. They might suggest that you join a committee dedicated to an area that you may find particularly interesting, like expanded wireless Internet access, better cafeteria food, or free newspapers on campus.

RUNNING FOR OFFICE

If you're campaigning for student government, the first thing to do is make yourself visible to everyone on campus! Go to meetings of every club that you can, and introduce yourself to its members. Tell them that you are running for a position and that you would greatly appreciate their vote. Next, make your posters and flyers memorable. The most successful candidates are the ones whose flyers catch people's eyes or make them laugh. Be creative and daring with your ideas and slogans (but remember to keep them appropriate).

WHAT IF YOU WANT TO BE THE PRESIDENT?

This is an ambition that many freshmen have when they first enter college. In order to achieve this goal, you must be heavily involved in student government from the outset. Apply for an appointed position your freshman year, within the executive board if possible. Talk to the current president and vice president and see what roles they played in the government during their early years on campus. Also, it is important to forge strong relationships with many different groups of people on campus, as well as with other members of the student government. Never underestimate the power an endorsement from another organization, or from other important student government leaders, can have on an election.

Being elected is about experience, vision, ideas, and having connections with as many different groups as you can. The entire student body elects you. That means that in order to win, people must believe that you care about all facets of the university, which can most easily be achieved by having alliances with many different clubs and organizations that stand for different issues.

Even if you don't win, the experience of campaigning is one-of-a-kind and will shape the person you become in the future. Don't get discouraged if you lose a race or aren't appointed to the position you want. There is always time to work your way up through the organization, and every step of the way is a blast!

SHY AWAY FROM THE SPOTLIGHT AT TIMES?

What if you don't like giving speeches in front of large crowds and don't want to be heavily burdened by one activity your freshman year? Luckily, there are many ways to get involved in behind-the-scenes capacities within student government. One great way not only to get involved, but also meet others in your same class, is to join a class committee. Generally appointed by the current administration, class committees are responsible for planning events for their specific class, conducting fund-raisers, and making sure that there is a strong camaraderie within their class. If your student government does not offer the option of the class committee, why not ask if you can start one? They are the perfect opportunity to meet other motivated people in your class while not taking an extremely public or time-consuming position.

And most important

Remember to have fun! Although student government can be demanding, it is extremely rewarding. You can see the effects of your work all around campus, which is immensely gratifying. Whether you launch an initiative to beautify campus through recycling or have free movies on Friday nights, student government allows for you to see what you have accomplished. If you are anything like me, you will catch the "student government bug" and want to be involved for all four years of college.

make a difference

Jessica Cruel, University of North Carolina—Chapel Hill

Your résumé is filled with accomplishments: internships, accolades, stellar GPA, and skills galore. But no volunteer activities? Even if you're no Mother Theresa, you should be volunteering! College is known as an arena for opportunity, a place of forward thinking and innovation, free love and revolution. Although career advancement is usually at the top of our list of reasons for volunteering (shallow, I know), there are other reasons to commit to helping others.

Making a difference in someone's life, whether in your own community or somewhere else in the world, is a great way to experience something you've never done before while promoting social welfare. Also, the things you can learn while volunteering can translate into life and job skills that improve your chances for snagging an internship or job that you really want.

The New Way to Travel: Voluntourism

Ikee Gardner, Duke University

While students have always done study abroad, it seems like more and more of my friends in college choose the volunteer route. In fact, I know girls who've done work in Mozambique, volunteered in South Africa, and rebuilt homes in New Orleans. It's called "voluntourism"— when people not originally from an area do a combination of tourist activities and volunteer work.

"I would do it again in a heartbeat. In fact, I probably will do it again," says Anita, a recent college grad, who volunteered in Belize last spring break. She helped rebuild a school, fixed and varnished furniture, put up drywall, and read to small children.

Where do voluntourists travel? Everywhere, from Uganda to France to New Orleans. Volunteers can do all kinds of activities depending on the location they choose—from building schools to teaching children English to working in wildlife preserves to working in hospitals and orphanages.

And it's not just students who volunteer. There are volunteer programs targeted to people over 50, teens, families, and working professionals. So if you decide to be a voluntourist, you can take your best friend, your little sister or brother, or your mom! Choosing whether to volunteer abroad can be a very big decision. Traditional study-abroad programs can usually give you academic credits toward graduation and/or give you a transcript from a foreign university.

However, voluntourism has unique perks that you can't get from a study-abroad program.

First, voluntouring is often more affordable. Study-abroad programs include tuition for classes, which can add up to thousands of dollars. It's often possible to do month-long volunteer programs for under $1,000.

Voluntouring can give you a realistic perspective on what life is like for the less fortunate in a specific country. You can do your part to help out the rest of the world. "It's too easy to point to a poor neighborhood and say, 'Oh, isn't that sad,' and then go back to the hotel and back to the States without doing anything," says Itohan, a junior who went to Belize with Anita. "I have two working hands and feet—so in essence, I have no excuse not to help!"

The great thing about voluntourism is that you never go it alone. Programs are often coordinated by foundations that have staff members traveling with the group. If you've never volunteered abroad before, they'll tell you what to do. Also, you still get to be a tourist! Itohan and Anita both saw the Mayan ruins while they were in Belize. Volunteering doesn't mean that you don't get to have fun.

Is volunteering abroad right for you? It's an incredibly rewarding experience. However, not everyone's cut out for it, especially if you're thinking of traveling to especially rural or obscure areas. Could you go to the bathroom on the ground or in grass? Could you live without electricity, hot water, phone, or Internet? If so, great! But if you can't live without a hot shower each morning, your makeup bag, and a cup of Starbucks, you might want to think again. Each program is different. Do your research.

Also, ask yourself this question: do you have skills or capabilities to contribute in the place you want to volunteer? For example, if you want to teach children English, are you a good teacher? Do you work well with kids? If so, go for it. If not, check out a different voluntourism program where you can make use of your special talents and skills.

Want to be a voluntourist? Check out websites like www.crossculturalsolutions.org and www.volunteerinternational.org. Or just type "international volunteering" into Google and see what pops up. Happy traveling!

MAKING A DIFFERENCE IN YOUR OWN BACKYARD

While there are many people throughout the rest of the world who are in need of help, you will also find people who need a hand in your own community. To make a difference in the world, sometimes it's as easy as getting in a car or bus to travel to a different city in the U.S. Check out AmeriCorps or City Year for some domestic volunteer opportunities. My friends that chose to rebuild homes for Katrina victims had an incredible experience. While they helped the survivors, they were also introduced to the fantastic culture, food, and music of New Orleans.

Something as simple as putting a smile on someone's face can be very contagious and truly change that person's outlook on life. Try volunteering at your local soup kitchen or spending time with the sick or elderly. These are perfect opportunities to gain insight into who you are as an individual as well as the truth about the state of American life.

I was able to witness this firsthand while delivering greetings and flowers at a hospital. The power of a balloon or a "Get Well Soon" card is immeasurable. Also, volunteering at a hospital is a great opportunity for those of you planning to go to medical or nursing school.

No matter what you end up doing, the perspective you will gain while helping others will change your outlook on life. To find these opportunities, see what your college has to offer. Most campuses have a community service office (some are even student-run) that connects students with local volunteer opportunities.

NOURISH THE FUTURE

Try being a role model for a child who needs one. You remember what it was like when you were young and had so many questions about life. Now imagine a child without access to successful and secure adults to help guide them along.

Teaching, tutoring, or mentoring a child can make a major difference in their lives. You can help decrease dropout and teen pregnancy rates. Girls have to deal with issues of self-image and sexual discovery at younger and younger ages. Help them understand what's happening and how to make the right decisions. Believe me—if you can handle the kids of today, then you can definitely deal with difficult coworkers in the future.

Where to look? If you are looking to make a difference in a child's life, try the local chapter of Boys & Girls Clubs of America or Teach for America, a two-year opportunity after graduation. Interested in law? Look into volunteering for CASA (Court Appointed Special Advocates—www.nationalcasa.org). The organization, which has grown to a network of more than 59,000 volunteers that serve 243,000 abused and neglected children nationwide, will train you to advocate on behalf of an abused child in a courtroom setting. This is an invaluable experience for someone interested in becoming a public interest lawyer.

SAVING MOTHER EARTH

You've heard it before: if we don't take efforts today to protect our precious ecosystem, the future does not look great for our children and the plants and animals with which we share this world. As one option for volunteerism, try getting engaged in activities that help protect our planet. It can be as simple as setting up recycling in your dorm or sorority house, or even becoming an activist by canvassing for Greenpeace or urging your congressional representative to support legislation that protects the environment.

Green is definitely the new pink!

If you are more hands-on in your desire to save the planet, go out and get local businesses and organizations to plant trees. Or even try to make your next vacation environmentally safe by going to the beach and saving the turtles. Green is definitely the new pink!

SUPPORT AN IMPORTANT CAUSE

The people we meet in our lives can have a major influence on our futures and our decision to volunteer. If your mother has breast cancer or your grandfather is suffering from Alzheimer's, why not get involved in a cause that works to end these diseases? An added benefit: helping the causes that mean a lot to your family can also bring you closer together.

You can do little things like buying an awareness tag or make greater commitments, like volunteering at the March of Dimes or the local American Cancer Society office. You can share a special bond with your fellow participants through similar stories of survival and suffering. The passion and motivation it takes to pursue and uplift a cause will enhance your life in so many ways.

HAVE FUN

No matter what you do, add some fun to the mix by inviting your friends to join you. Skip the spring break trip to Panama City and instead go with friends on a trip to California to work for Save the Whales. This experience still includes lots of sun and waves, and can offer much more as far as bonding is concerned.

U Chic Tip!

Remember that volunteering doesn't have to be a drag. Going with groups can actually be loads of fun. You get to see another side of friends, and it can also be a great opportunity to make memories that will truly last a lifetime. I'll never forget shelving dented cans with friends at our local Salvation Army "Grocery Store" and getting rid of the outdated fashions in their closet.

Family members especially make great volunteer companions, so suggest it for the next family reunion or when Mom is complaining that you don't spend enough time at home.

You will also meet many new people you may have never run into otherwise when you choose to volunteer. Who knows, you may come out of a volunteer experience with an entirely new group of friends.

No matter what your background—whether you were born with a silver spoon or not—it's time to get out of your comfort zone to see how others live and think. Pushing yourself to do things you would normally shy away from will help you to gain perspective on what is really important in life.

tips for the busy student athlete

*Krista Naposki, Elon University and
Amanda Sandlin, Rider University*

S tudent athletes live very different lives than the rest of the student body. From 6 a.m. lifting sessions to 6-hour bus trips, time is precious for this segment of the population. Student athletes at every level must carefully balance their sports with academics, relationships, and their careers. It requires a huge commitment, but it also generates great rewards. Here are some tips for the busy student athlete looking to stay on top.

TIP 1: KNOW YOUR PRIORITIES
Life as a student athlete is different from that of the regular student. When you leave home you might think that you are "on your own" and completely free to do anything you can imagine, but that is not necessarily the case if you're playing college sports. Many

times, coaches can be just as strict as parents. Like your parents, your coach is not going to want to hear that you've been in trouble for underage drinking or public drunkenness, or that your grades are falling. This is probably one of the most important aspects of being a student athlete. You have to respect what your coach tells you to do. He or she expects your all. Your team expects your all.

Also, understand that your school expects more from you than from the majority of the student body. You represent the university and are expected to act appropriately. This includes Facebook and partying. Be responsible, or your scholarship could be at stake.

TIP 2: ACADEMICS MATTER GREATLY

One of the most important aspects of being a student athlete is your grades. If your grades slip too low, you could be held on academic probation. The easiest way to avoid this is to simply go to class. I knew a girl that always waited until the last minute to get her assignments done. Her procrastination didn't pay off: she ended up with a GPA lower than the academic standards and got kicked off the team. It can happen to anyone, so be sure to keep your grades up. And remember, just like the NCAA commercial says, "Most college athletes go pro in something other than sports."

Why I Quit

I quit playing soccer for my college team just after my junior year season had wrapped up. Every time people ask me why I quit with just one year left, I respond one of two ways: "It's not just the senior year season. It's the spring season. It's summer training. It's preseason. I just could not invest all my efforts into that single activity for one more year." Or, "There were too many opportunities I was missing out on. I just enjoy other things. I had a spring term internship. I enjoy being active in a sorority, working on my school newspaper, and going on weekend vacations."

Do I regret playing college soccer? No: I had great teammates and I needed the structure for the majority of my college career. There are no excuses for falling behind when you're on a tight student athlete's schedule, because you just can't. But eventually, I grew out of the desire to play every day, to attend numerous athletic events, and to be held back from other things. The sport I had played since age four had turned into an obligation, not a passion.

TIP 3: VALUE YOUR HEALTH

Make sure to get adequate sleep, eat healthy, and relax. This is important for your sport, but it is also important for your general health. If you don't sleep enough, your playing will suffer, your academics will suffer, and you will probably be upset. Athletes expend a lot of calories, so make sure you eat often and eat healthy. Relaxation is also important. Take the time to slow down and have some time to yourself.

TIP 4: HAVE FRIENDS BOTH ON AND OFF THE TEAM

There is much to be said about expanding your circle of friends. Since you spend so much of your time dedicated to sports, it can be a great stress relief to just chill with friends that have no connection to sports whatsoever. Having trouble meeting people? Join a club or two that meshes well with your practices, but be sure not to overload your schedule. Also, there is always the option of joining a sorority. Sororities, in general, are eager to recruit women that are actively involved on campus and in sports, and are, therefore, willing to work around a busy student athlete's schedule.

Now, I am not saying that you shouldn't be close with those on your team. Your team is practically your family, and with every family comes occasional drama and issues that develop. Cliques will form. But there is good news! You can be one of those rare people that is friends with everyone. Certainly, one can't avoid all conflicts, but it is possible to stay out of most petty arguments by simply refusing to feed into it.

TIP 5: ENJOY!

As a student athlete, your life may be stressful, but sometimes it helps to remember why you play the sport in the first place. As kids, we started playing sports for fun and friends. These two things should still matter most. And it they don't, you should think about doing something else.

U Chic Essentials—Getting Involved

Follow your passion

Get involved in activities that come naturally to you and get you excited. You'll be more apt to stick with them, and even aim for the all-important leadership roles in the group. Don't be swayed too much by popularity.

Beware the buffet effect

Does the following scenario sound familiar? You're at a buffet and the many delectables entice a greater appetite than you really have. Ah, if only you had enjoyed just one or two of the items that caught your eye. Getting involved on campus can lead to a similar buffet effect. Try hard to limit your activities to your favorite few, and you'll be able to dedicate more time and receive more enjoyment from them.

College is your testing ground

What you learn outside of class can often be more important than what you learn inside. So get out, and get involved! Getting involved on campus or in your community is one of your best opportunities to test the skills that are most important in the real world. And don't be afraid to take the lead early on. By getting out of your comfort zone, you're building experience and getting your name out there as a go-to person.

Looking for more great advice? Head to www.UniversityChic.com and look for "U Chic Picks!" for our fav resources and websites—they come highly recommended from our guide's contributors and editors. Be sure to leave your suggestions as well!

CHAPTER 5

Tech Etiquette for a Facebook Age

S hould I ask the hottie in History for his number or should I just friend him on Facebook?"

"Is it OK to break up with someone via text message?"

"Should I text my new love interest or is a phone call more appropriate?"

"Am I spending too much time on Facebook? Am I an addict?"

Do any of these questions sound familiar?

With iPhones, BlackBerrys, and Facebook, socializing is a whole lot easier these days. But with this ease comes the added stress of knowing *when* is the right time to use *which* form of communication. Also, you can almost forget the importance of in-person interaction every now and then.

To provide some much-needed rules of engagement, read on for some fail-proof tech etiquette for a Facebook age.

to call or text: communication rules for dating

Erica Strauss, Kent State University

ollege life comes complete with an array of attractive, educated people at your disposal. Throw in some alcohol, coed dorms, and an ever-growing list of Facebook event invites, and you've got yourself one crazy dating scene. It seems like there are no real rules, and if there are, people sure aren't afraid to bend—or completely break—them.

Let's set the scene. You meet an adorable, delicious boy at a house party, complete with his astrological sign tattooed on his bronzed bicep (and, of course, you totally check your horoscope like every day). You engage in a heated discussion about all your other interests (finally, a guy who will admit to loving reality TV!), and find that you have a lot in common. You're really into each other, so you exchange numbers and go home happy, elated even.

However, it's the next morning and the dilemma sets in. You have his number, now what? What's a modern girl to do when

she has two completely viable options for communication—
to call or to text? And there is always Facebook to complicate
things further.

WHEN TO CALL

If you have something serious to talk about

My number one pet peeve is when people—girlfriends and
boyfriends alike—decide to initiate a fight, debate, or other
meaningful discussion via text message. In the age of texting,
sometimes it's easy to forget that some conversations are supposed
to be long, drawn-out, and, above all else, meaningful. There
are still certain situations, especially in dating, that require you
to actually use your voice—and not a keyboard or cell phone
keypad—to express yourself. Even if we're talking about your
boyfriend of three years, he deserves the chance to actually hear
what you have to say.

Also, text messages can be easily misinterpreted when trying
to discuss something where emotions are involved—those little
smiley faces do not tell all! Sarcasm and other voice inflections are
often misread in text messages, causing a whole mess of confusion
between the two parties involved. There have been numerous
occasions when girls have misread text messages and caused lots
of unnecessary drama with boyfriends. If you really want to ensure
he understands why you freaked out the night before, discuss the
events over the phone, if not in person!

If you aren't distracted

My ex-boyfriend and I attempted to carry on many a phone conversation when I lived in the dorm. Let me tell you—living around 40 girls did not make for optimum relationship communication time. If you want to chat it up with that new boy in your life or have a quality phone date with your current BF, make sure you are somewhere quiet, free of giggling girls chugging wine and/or discussing the latest celeb gossip. Devote your concentration to the conversation and really listen to what your beau is saying. You'll be surprised how much you will enjoy talking with your sweetie when you give him your full attention.

If you want to make plans

It's tempting to ask your guy to hang in a text message; but wait until you show up at one movie theater and he accidentally goes to another. Confirming when, where, and how you and your dude are going to meet up is best done through verbal communication and will help avoid confusion later. It's faster than waiting for a text message response, which as we all know can take hours—if you get one at all. Make special plans more solid over the phone.

If you want to show that you're truly interested

When you take the time out of your obviously super-busy schedule to actually dial your crush's number, it shows that you have a genuine interest in him and what he has to say. Although firing off a short "What's up?" text is quick and painless, it does not say much, literally.

If you want to break it off

Don't commit the cardinal sin of college dating—the text message breakup. Although I don't think that having a "You-were-the-best-and-worst-thing-that-ever-happened-to-me" tear-jerking conversation over the phone is much better, it at least gives the other person an opportunity to defend himself and spill his side of the story. Breakups aren't easy no matter how you have to handle them, but a phone conversation is a much more civil way to move on.

WHEN TO TEXT

If he texts first

Take the scenario where you meet at a party. We can argue that chivalry is dead, but let's be honest here—you know that any guy who is truly interested in hanging out with your fabulous self will soon send you a quick, flirty text or call you up to take you out (or at the very least, invite you to tag along to a frat party). If the cute boy texts you first, a text response is not only a way to show that you, too, are interested, but it's also polite. Manners are always classy; and classy is always attractive.

If you're super busy, duh

College students are constantly swamped with papers, 300-page readings on thrilling subjects like the principles of formal logic,

45-minute presentations, what have you. Between all your activities, it might be hard to find the time for a phone call—especially if you just want to check up. Sending a friendly "How's it going?" or "I love you!" text message—depending on the situation, of course—is totally acceptable. In fact, it might even be the perfect way to go—especially if your partner is busy, too! You can also use text messages as a way to arrange times to communicate other ways. Send a quick "Call me after six!" text message if you miss a call during class so your sweetheart knows you aren't too busy or completely ignoring him.

If you're already in a relationship

The rules change quite a bit when you're already attached. While you still shouldn't use the text message as an easy way out (like to break up) or as a way to tackle some serious drama, text messages are a good way to communicate with someone you already know and love. They know your style of speech, they know how your brain works (or at least attempt to understand it), and they will have a better idea about how to decipher your text messages than someone you just met. And when it comes to social networking sites like Facebook and MySpace? It might be OK to occasionally post on your BF's wall, or send him a cute message that you think will brighten his day—but delving into anything too serious using the Internet is an absolutely terrible idea. It's there forever, for the whole world to see.

Remember that while phone calls and text messages are great ways to communicate with the opposite sex, face-to-face encounters are ideal. In order to establish a real connection, you have to be able to see, hear, and touch the other person. No text message could ever replace a good snuggle session on your comfy couch or a romantic dinner at your favorite sushi restaurant. It's easy to stumble in the fast-paced dating world of BlackBerrys, YouTube, Google, text messages, iPods, you name it. But with proper tech etiquette, new technologies can make your love life a whole lot easier and more interesting.

blirting 101: socializing via blackberry

Johannah Cornblatt, Harvard University

(Owner of BlackBerry 8830 World Edition with pink sleeve)

For college girls juggling classes, extracurriculars, and boys, a BlackBerry has become the trendiest campus accessory around. If you're college-bound, you're probably thinking about getting/begging for one (if you're not already). With students toting these handheld companions from libraries to bars, flirting via BlackBerry—or "blirting," as it's called—has revolutionized college courtships. While learning how to operate one of these smartphones is fairly easy, navigating your way through the new communication etiquette is no simple task. Here's what you should know before investing in this expensive toy:

D & R

Ever wonder if your crush listened to that voicemail you left yet? Well, BlackBerrys have brought the drama of delayed responses to a whole new level. The angst stems from two tiny letters—*D* and *R*—which indicate, respectively, whether a BlackBerry message (BBM) has been delivered or received. If you read a BBM and don't respond, count on that *R* insulting your contact.

Ping!!!

If contacts don't respond instantly, you can try getting their attention with a feature called ping. It's sort of like banging on a door after you knocked politely. If you're comfortable enough to pound on someone's door in real life, then go ahead and ping. If not, hold your thumbs.

Identity Theft

One click on "edit my info" is essentially all it takes for someone to change their display name to yours. I learned that the hard way after a guy I liked began receiving lewd BBMs from his friend, who had changed his display name to mine. In order to avoid this aggravation, it's a good idea to establish codes with your closest contacts to confirm your identity.

Group Chats

These are great for coordinating study groups, extracurricular meetings, or just trips to the dining hall. Chat with caution, though. Here, too, people can falsely represent themselves by changing their display name.

Voice Note

Miss your long-distance boyfriend or your high school friends? You can also exchange brief voice messages with your BBM contacts. Don't get too lovey-dovey, though. Unlike voicemails, voice notes automatically play on speakerphone.

Snooping

My friend once suspected her boyfriend of cheating and, sure enough, she found incriminating BBMs from another girl while he was in the bathroom. Although you may log out of your gmail account compulsively, don't forget that your handheld computer holds similarly private info. Try password-protecting your device, and watch where you put it down. This is good for other things besides cheating on your boyfriend, of course.

BlackBerry Praying

That's what cynics call the classic head-bowed, hands-cupped position of BlackBerry addicts. It's not a pose you want to strike in class, and some of my friends have gone as far as issuing a ban on "praying" during meals.

BlackBerry Neck & BlackBerry Thumb

With users hunched over their BlackBerrys 24/7, sore necks and thumbs are two of the latest maladies pervading college campuses. Try a Bluetooth headset to take the stress off your neck, and throw a ring finger in every now and then to give those thumbs a break.

facebook's dark side

Nisha Chittal, University of Illinois–Urbana-Champaign

No longer exclusive to college students, Facebook.com is one of the fastest-growing social networking websites today. It's just how college students communicate. In fact, the Facebook epidemic has reached the point that it is strange when you meet someone in college who *doesn't* have a Facebook profile; one wonders why they would choose not to partake in the Facebook fun.

> ### Did You Know?
>
> In 2006, about 3 in 4 college students had a Facebook account.

Not long ago, many experts felt that spending large amounts of time using the Internet for social interaction was a sign of a personal deficiency in social skills. In other words, people who spent a lot of time socially networking online were doing it because they felt socially awkward face-to-face. However, in the rapidly evolving world of online communications, such generalizations are no longer accurate. Today's students have integrated online communication like Facebook and other social networking sites into our daily lives to enrich, rather than replace, our already existing relationships. But like anything else, it has its drawbacks as well.

YOUR PROFILE SAYS IT ALL

The average college student logs into their Facebook account nearly every day, spending anywhere from 10 minutes to 3 hours a day checking out the latest details on their friends' profiles. There are even categories of Facebook users determined by the number of "friends" that one has prominently displayed on the front page of one's profile. If you've got under 200, then consider yourself a casual Facebook user, one who thinks it is fun but doesn't quite see its full potential so doesn't waste too much time on it. Have 200–300 friends? You're the average Facebook user, one who probably checks their account and exchanges wall posts with their friends at least once a day. For those entertaining 300–400+ friends, congrats. You're popular, one who makes lot of friends and acquaintances and uses Facebook to keep in touch with all of them. But 500+? You've entered new territory—desperate. Let me guess: you are one of those people who Facebooks everyone, even when you haven't met the person yet!

For all of the benefits that Facebook provides, however—like keeping in touch with friends (and especially when you're wanting to procrastinate)—Facebook does have its dark side as well.

WHO CAN SEE YOUR PROFILE?

By now, you've surely heard the stories on how potential employers search for you on social-networking websites like Facebook and have made hiring decisions based on what they find. These stories are true. Those fun party pics with you and your drunk friends might not work for future employers. However, college students are entitled to partake in a little fun with their friends, and there's no reason you shouldn't have pictures to document the memories. But you should always take precautions with *what* you post on Facebook.

U Chic Tip! Don't Post It All

With the variety of individuals on Facebook today—parents, employers, university faculty members, and even police officers—it is important to censor what you post. A safe rule of thumb is to not post anything you wouldn't want your parents or boss to see.

If—for whatever reason—you must post the pictures, exercise caution. Use the "limited profile" feature, and use it liberally. If you must be Facebook friends with someone who you'd rather not have viewing your entire profile—say a parent, younger sibling, boss, etc.—be careful here. I, for one, am Facebook friends with my company's executive director. I immediately put her on "limited" to make sure she cannot see any pictures or anything else she could possibly deem inappropriate for a member of her staff.

Also, make sure to use other privacy restrictions like only allowing your friends to view your profile. Many students are now even making their Facebook profiles completely "unsearchable" so that employers cannot check their Facebook profile during the recruitment season. Last important tip: you can also block specific individuals from seeing your profile. Certainly, the technology will continue to change while you're in college. Be sure to keep up on these changes to make sure that you are not jeopardizing any future opportunities with a little bit of totally normal college debauchery.

DOES FACEBOOK CONTROL YOU?

If you worry that you might qualify as a Facebook addict, then you most likely have a problem. Interested in changing? Try documenting for a couple days how often you go on Facebook and how much time you spend on the site during each visit. You might be shocked to learn how much time you waste each day reading up on the details of the lives of your friends and acquaintances. Once you have a good feel for the average amount of time you waste on Facebook, substitute this time with something more positive like going to the gym, meditation, yoga, or spending time with your good friends *in person*. I'm not saying that the solution is to give Facebook up entirely. We all know that's an impossible suggestion.

But just try finding some balance in your life and you'll feel a lot better for it.

Did You Know?

A recent poll by Sophos (an IT firm) of 500 full-time employees who are recent college graduates found that 14.8% of them admitted to being logged onto Facebook virtually all day during work, and another 8% admitted to checking their Facebook up to 10 times a day at work!

"The results show that more than one fifth of these Facebook users are actually Facebook abusers. They're seriously struggling to tear themselves away from the website when they should be concentrating on their jobs—disturbing news for all organizations that are still allowing employees uncontrolled access," said Graham Cluley, senior technology consultant at Sophos, in an article for the *Kansas City InfoZine*.

FACEBOOK AND DATING

Facebook has changed the way our generation perceives relationships and interpersonal communication, and that's not necessarily always a good thing. What happens when you're going on a first date with someone, and are only pretending to learn new things about them from your conversations, since you've already memorized their favorite movies and TV shows from their Facebook profile? What you can learn about someone from staring at a computer does not, and should not, in any way, replace interacting with them "IRL."

In the age of the emoticon, people claim that online communication makes dating and friendships easier, but actually, when you look deeper, it can be an obstacle to our ability to interact with people in person. It's easy to come up with witty one-liners online, but more important to be able to improvise in person. Facebook is fun, but can take a lot away from the process of getting to know another person one-on-one. Don't let this happen to you.

MAINTAINING STRONG FRIENDSHIPS

An interesting blog, Employee Evolution (www.employeeevolution. com), claims that social-networking sites like Facebook are perpetuating weak ties and fewer strong relationships. Why? Essentially, the problem lies in how easy it is to become "friends" with someone. Within one meeting and a couple clicks of a mouse, you can be listed as someone's "friend," but does this really translate to a friendship? Does writing a happy birthday message on their wall once a year really mean you're buddies in the real world? I don't think so. Maintaining a friendship with someone requires a lot more effort than a once-a-year wall post lost among hundreds of others.

On the flip side, according to Wikipedia, social networks are great because they help us create lots of ties and get access to new information that we wouldn't otherwise have access to while allowing us to keep in touch with our closer friends.

But never forget that it's also easy for those who were once close friends to be relegated to weak online acquaintances. Make sure not to let networking sites like Facebook overtake your social life, and don't forget to maintain your friendships offline as well! When you no longer see someone in class everyday or are too busy to hang out with them, it's easy to substitute the occasional wall post or message saying hello, but this is not a good replacement for spending time together in person and won't help build your relationships.

PARTING WORDS OF ADVICE

Facebook is a fun and extremely useful tool—there are plenty of people you might otherwise lose touch with in life that Facebook will allow you to keep in touch with—but like anything else, use it in moderation. Because I know how addictive Facebook can be, during finals week each year I usually let a friend log into my account and change my password so that I don't log back into Facebook until after exams are over. It's just one extra way of making sure Facebook doesn't interfere with what is important to me…like doing well on an exam! Don't let it take over—if you find yourself spending large amounts of time memorizing people's profiles or commenting on photos the night before you have a major history paper due, don't forget your priorities and log off of that site!

U Chic Essentials—Tech Etiquette for a Facebook Age

Build the relationship in person

Remember that while phone calls and text messages are great ways to communicate with the opposite sex, face-to-face encounters are ideal. In order to establish a real connection, you have to be able to see, hear, and touch the other person. No text message could ever replace a good snuggle session on your comfy couch or romantic dinner at your favorite sushi restaurant.

Don't post it all

With the variety of individuals on Facebook today, it's important to use good judgment about what you do and do not post online.

Save the important stuff for in-person

In the age of texting, sometimes it's easy to forget that some conversations are supposed to be face-to-face and meaningful. Dating in particular calls for real conversations.

Looking for more great advice? Head to www.UniversityChic.com and look for "U Chic Picks!" for our fav resources and websites—they come highly recommended from our guide's contributors and editors. Be sure to leave your suggestions as well!

CHAPTER 6

Love Life

*I*t's rare to find a woman in college these days whose primary goal is to get hitched. But it wasn't too long ago that some women went to college solely for their Mrs. degree. Of course serious relationships still exist in college these days. It's just the way we approach and view dating has radically changed.

So what to expect? From short-term relationships to long-term relationships to an occasional hookup and possibly even dormcest (aka "dating around the dorm"), be prepared for *anything* when it comes to dating in college. To give you a crash course on the college dating scene, we've pulled together some essential dating advice from college women nationwide. Having been there and pretty much done everything you can imagine when it comes to dating, these women have much to share!

the scoop on the college dating scene

Jillian E. Sorgini, Hofstra University

*L*et's face it. After you've said good-bye to your parents and finished unpacking, what you're really excited to check out is *not* the campus or your classes.

But as much as I wanted to meet a cute guy and establish a long-term and stable relationship in college, that was not my sole motivation for going to school. After all, this is the age of the independent woman. As an independent woman, you're here to make your dreams your reality, and finding a man should not be your first goal in mind. It's just an added bonus, icing on the cake, when you meet that special someone in college.

Since the rules of dating have changed drastically (even since your older sister was in college), I wanted to share a little advice on how to enjoy the college dating scene without losing sight of yourself, your goals, or your future.

STAY TRUE TO YOURSELF

Let's start with the don'ts: *don't date just to be like your friends.* Before you start dating, make sure you do it for the right reasons. I'm sure your parents have told you time and time again to always act for the right reasons, and now being on your own, it's time to test out your ability to stay true to yourself. Don't make decisions about your own love life based on what your friends are doing. Even if all of them are dating, this does not mean that you have to enter the dating pool. Also, having a boyfriend will not prove anything to yourself or your friends about your maturity or self-worth.

Don't set out looking for a boyfriend. It's so easy to get caught up in a relationship and have your social life revolve around him rather than to make your own friends. And if it doesn't work out, you'll regret not taking the time to make connections with others when you're sitting at home alone in your dorm room trying to recover from a breakup. In college, especially, there are so many new people to meet and interesting opportunities that it can be a bit overwhelming at first. But what should be first and foremost on your new agenda are your friendships. Take the time to get to know your girlfriends before you call anyone your boyfriend. After all, guys come and go. Some may even break your heart, but after all is said and done, your girlfriends will stand by your side through it all.

A friend of mine and her boyfriend broke up after a two-year relationship. They met right when they came to campus, hit it off, and jumped right into a relationship. For two years, her life revolved around him, and she lost touch with many of her friends. When her relationship fell apart, it was hard for a lot of her friends to be there for her since she had cast them aside in favor of her boyfriend. It took some time, but eventually she earned back the trust of all her friends. Her breakup was hard to deal with, but it opened her eyes to the fact that there is always more than one important person in your life.

> But what should be first and foremost on your new agenda are your friendships. Take the time to get to know your girlfriends before you call anyone your boyfriend. After all, guys come and go. Some may even break your heart, but after all is said and done, your girlfriends will stand by your side through it all.

GETTING STARTED

OK, so I'm done with the don'ts. Once you've made your friends and you are ready to take the plunge into the dating pool, who can you date and where do you meet them?

BOYFRIEND MATERIAL

When starting to date someone, ideally, you want to start with a clean slate. You shouldn't have to pick up the pieces from a previous dating disaster. Guys without girlfriends—meaning they are single but also over any previous girlfriends—are your prime dating material. While everyone comes with their own baggage, fresh baggage is not fun to deal with. It takes time to get over any relationship and the solution is not to jump right into the next.

On the flip side, sometimes guys are just not ready for dating. Not everyone comes to college with the maturity level it takes to be in a meaningful relationship, and the unfortunate truth is that girls mature faster than guys, and some guys still have not caught up even by college.

Another problem you may come across is that some guys are, at times, only looking to hook up. They aren't looking to get into anything serious right away since they are still trying to figure out exactly what they want out of a relationship—almost like window-shopping. But hooking up with someone—with the hope of eventually dating—never really works out the way you want. While there is nothing wrong with wanting to date or wanting a commitment from a guy, you have to be up-front about your needs from the very beginning. Otherwise, you may soon discover that you've been wasting your time on the wrong person, and no one likes feeling that they've wasted time.

WHERE *NOT* TO MEET

At this point, classes can seem like the perfect place to meet someone, but mixing business and pleasure can be a difficult duo. Dating someone you share a class with could work against you—if you break up, you'll still see each other every day. Even dating someone with the same major can be dangerous. My school is by no means a large one, so every year I have the same drama majors in my classes. It's not like you can stop going to classes or really avoid seeing them. I have friends that have dated people with the same major and when it doesn't work out, it can get ugly. The choice is yours to make, but be sure there is a solid connection between you and your fellow cutie of a classmate before you start dating.

BEING A GROUPIE IS NOT THE WAY TO GO

At all cost, avoid becoming a groupie. Let me describe the typical scene: hanging around at the same place every single weekend with the same group of guys and girls. During my freshman year, my friends and I hung out at one of the sports houses (like a fraternity house for a sport team) every night. We pigeonholed ourselves into the category of girls who only date jocks, which couldn't be further from the truth. Only one of my friends was actually dating a jock; the rest of us just considered ourselves friends with the guys. But not everyone seemed to believe that, including non-jocks that we were interested in. Once we realized that everyone looked at us as groupies, we got smart and quickly switched up our hangouts. It was too soon in our college career to be affiliated with only one group and, besides, jocks don't have the greatest reputations when it comes to dating. Fortunately, we only spent one semester as "groupies" and no long-term damage was done to our reputations.

MORE ON THE SUBJECT OF REPUTATIONS

If there is one piece of advice I could give that you should take to heart, it's that your reputation is extremely important in college, especially at a smaller school. While your college may be bigger than your high school, people still gossip and word does travel. Now, you know that there will always be petty gossip that you just brush off, but when even your closest friends show concern for you, it may be time to take a step back and reflect on what you're doing. Some of us can go a little crazy with our newfound sense of independence and make decisions that we eventually regret. If you come to college fresh out of a breakup and start sleeping around, it can definitely damage your reputation. But don't worry; nothing is permanent. As soon as you realize that you aren't happy with choices you're making, start making better ones. Your reputation may stick for a little while, but once you start making changes, your reputation will change as well.

WHERE TO MEET THE RIGHT GUYS

So at this point I'm sure you are wondering where you will meet someone to date. For the most part, many of the guys that my friends and I have dated we met through our friends. Classes *outside* your major area of interest can be a safe place to meet guys as well. Maybe you could take an interesting elective class to see who else is in it. Extracurricular activities afford another opportunity—just beware if it is an activity where you spend a lot of time together. Don't be afraid to put yourself out there.

Sporting events and off-campus bars or local cafes are good as well. Make an effort to search out a place that fits your style.

Ever heard of dormcest? Perhaps the most overlooked location for dating is your own housing building. We've all heard about the girl-next-door, but what about the guy-next-door? It certainly is convenient to hook up with someone who lives in the same dorm. You don't have to worry about what to bring over, it's a short walk, especially if the weather is bad, and the walk of shame is minimized. On the other hand, once it's over it can be hard to avoid that person. Chances are you will still bump into them, and even worse, they could be with someone new when you see them next. So before you become friendly with the guy-next-door, make sure you can handle seeing him with someone else.

In college, the only real dating rules are those that you make for yourself. There are no parents to check up on you and enforce a curfew. What you choose to do is completely up to you, so set some rules for yourself and be picky about whom you decide to date. When I say picky, I am not talking about only dating blondes or athletes. I am talking about setting standards for yourself.

U Chic Tip!

Don't date someone if you have to justify your relationship to all your friends. It's not a good sign when you have to give your friends a fair warning before they meet him.

WHAT YOU CAN EXPECT TO RUN INTO

Predicting what you'll experience in the world of college dating is just as tricky as predicting the weather. There are times when you'll bask in the sunlight of a new relationship. Other times you'll muddle your way through murky waters of ambiguity. And don't forget about the storms. You have to prepare for the unexpected.

Open relationships

Perhaps it's human nature, but we usually want what we can't have. You know the "grass is always greener on the other side" phenomenon. This is especially true when dealing with guys with girlfriends. For your own sake, stay away from the guy with the girlfriend back home. Even if he is in an "open relationship," getting involved with him is just asking for trouble. First of all, the term "open relationship" is a bit of an oxymoron. "Relationship" implies monogamy while "open" does not. If you want to avoid any future drama, be sure to stay away from these guys.

If you do decide to date a person in an open relationship, try not to get too attached. Chances are that if it comes down to choosing between you and his girlfriend, he will choose his girlfriend. No matter how fun or pretty you are, you have to admit that it makes sense; he has more history with her and is more comfortable. I have been in this situation once before and the best advice I can give is to run away if a guy mentions that his relationships aren't monogamous.

What happens when you want more? Here's a little tale to illustrate. I wasn't looking for any kind of relationship, but one night while out with friends I met a really great guy, or so I thought. We had similar interests and hit it off right away. Unfortunately, he and his girlfriend, who was at school in a different state, were having problems. They decided to be in an open relationship. This is the point where I should have walked away, but I thought I had a chance at something with this guy. To make matters worse, he pursued me as if there were no one else in the picture, randomly surprising me, having dinner with me, and basically all the stuff you do when you like someone. Ultimately, he and his girlfriend worked things out and I was crushed. He even had the audacity to tell me that if things didn't work out this time with her, maybe we could give it a shot. As much as I hoped that would happen, I had to make the decision to not date someone that would always consider me second-best.

Rebounders

Like I said earlier, be careful or even steer clear of anyone who has recently gotten out of a relationship. They are on the rebound, and it might be at your expense. There is no set amount of time that it takes a person to get over someone. Depending on the individual, it can range anywhere from one week to three months or even more. Some guys never get over their ex-girlfriends! Make sure whomever you start to date is still not hung up on his ex—if he's constantly talking about her or comparing you to her, it's best to let him be. To be fair, sometimes he may not even know he's constantly talking about her. Speak up and make him aware of it. When it comes down to it, he shouldn't have to choose his memories over you. But, if he seems to wish his past memories were his present life, it is best to move on.

Fraternity guys and athletes

To set the record straight, frat boys, athletes, and the like are sometimes at a disadvantage. It seems that they are always portrayed in a bad light. A close friend of mine is dating a guy in a fraternity, and true, at times, it can be frustrating. When there is drama between her and her boyfriend, it seems the whole frat knows about it and she becomes "the bitch." On the other hand, there is something to be said for stereotypes; they don't come out of nowhere. My motto is to give everyone a chance. More often than not, guys will surprise you.

In all honesty, when it comes to dating in college, you will most likely meet someone when you least expect it. Maybe they live next door to your best friend or maybe you will meet them at a party. No matter what the situation, just be yourself and live up to your own expectations. The rest will follow suit!

long-distance love

Erica Strauss, Kent State University

I fell in love for the first time when I was 16. His name was Ryan and he was everything I wanted at that age: passionate, dark, addicted to punk music and cigarettes.

We were high school sweethearts, the couple that made everyone sick with incessant hand-holding and kissing in the hallways. We were inseparable for five years to be exact. And when the day came that I had to squeeze all my belongings into my parents' minivan and head across the state, I knew that it meant leaving him, and completely changing the dynamics of our once perfect romance. I had to face up to a harsh reality after I started to call Kent State University home. Long-distance relationships take some serious effort, and sometimes it isn't worth it. I had to learn firsthand the ins and outs of what makes a long-distance relationship work— and what can cause it to crumble.

Whether you're trying to make the transition from high school sweethearts to committed college lovers, or you met someone from another university or even another country, having your sweetie miles away is never easy. So, what can you do to make it work? And if it's not working, how do you decide to move on?

REALIZE THAT IT WILL BE HARD WORK

First and foremost, realize that in a long-distance relationship, you will experience challenges that new couples in college don't. Sure, you will have to tackle issues of trust, jealousy, and intimacy—just like any couple—but you can't just make it all better with a goodnight kiss. However, all is not lost; your relationship can survive. Just make sure from the very beginning of the separation that both you and your partner are ready to expend the extra energy that comes with making a long-distance commitment.

ESTABLISH BOUNDARIES

An important word of advice: your lover might see a long-distance relationship as the perfect way to have his cake and eat it, too. Don't let this happen to you unless you are OK with sharing your guy. Make sure that both of you are clear about the way the relationship is supposed to work. Are you going to remain exclusive or will you be allowed to date other people? If you meet someone you feel you might have a better connection with, will you remain friends? These are just a few of the many issues you'll want to address before the separation. If you take the time to be up-front about the relationship from the get-go, this prevents confusion and possible heartbreak later.

TRUST YOUR PARTNER

Once the boundaries are set, you then have to *let go*—not of your guy but of your tendency to worry or not trust your partner. Yes, this one seems obvious, but when distance becomes a factor in an otherwise super-sweet relationship, the equation changes quite a bit. In order for your LDR to work, there has to be a very high level of trust.

DON'T BUG YOUR BEAU WITH ENDLESS PHONE CALLS

Demanding that he or she tell you where they are every second of every day will do nothing but tear you, and your relationship, apart. You both are in a new place and an exciting time of your life. Let him—and yourself—grow, learn, and have fun without a cell phone glued to the ear. Besides, no one really likes the girl who sits in the corner on the phone with her boy all night. Plus, you'll have much more to say when you can finally talk with your guy without distractions.

BE HONEST ABOUT YOUR WEEKEND PLANS

Don't tell your partner you plan to sit at home on a Friday night if you're ready to waltz your way to the local hangouts in your brand-new Manolos. Even though my BF and I were miles apart, I couldn't bring myself to tell him what I was really doing, and sometimes I'd ignore his phone calls on Friday night just to avoid a fight. I found out the hard way that this breeds mistrust in a relationship; every time I didn't answer, he assumed I was doing something I shouldn't be. He never cared if I hung out with other guys—he cared about me and wanted me to enjoy college—but by me not being honest, I created a pretty sticky situation. By avoiding his phone calls, I created an issue that was hard to resolve.

LEARN TO TRUST YOURSELF

Do you think you can resist the temptation of going home with the cute boy at the bar after a few Jäegerbombs? Don't put yourself, or your partner, in the position to get hurt. It's always OK to go out, in fact that's one of the amazing qualities about an LDR: you can still maintain your freedom. But if you're constantly tempted to go home with someone else, or always want to go out "just in case" you meet Mr. Right, you need to reevaluate your current relationship. It's natural to miss the closeness that comes with a regular relationship, and you might be eyeballing that hottie just because you miss your own. But if you go out with the sole intention of meeting someone new, you probably just need to break it off with your current beau.

AND IF YOU DO MEET SOMEONE ELSE OR FEEL TEMPTED TO CHEAT—DON'T!

Break it off with your partner before you start romancing another student. My LDR came to an end toward the end of my sophomore year. I had finally started to feel comfortable around a certain group of people—I found my niche, if you will. I also started to get a little too comfortable with a boy in this group of friends. I noticed that I would get more excited when he called or sent me a cute text than when my own boyfriend did. I knew that this was a sign that I needed to talk to my BF and decide what to do about it. It was crazy—I called him to talk about my feelings for the other boy and he had a very similar situation for him at home. So we decided, very mutually, to leave the relationship behind. This communication between us at the time of our breakup has made it possible for us to become friends (after a good nine months of no communication whatsoever!). Honesty really is the best policy, and I'm so glad that I was honest with my boy at the time.

COMMUNICATE

Communication is key in every relationship—but people in LDRs have to be a little more creative in their approach to keeping in touch. My long-distance boyfriend was a little short on cash, so even though we were only 2½ hours apart, weekend visits were not always an option. I missed his forehead kisses, his calloused hands; I even missed riding around in his disgusting car while he blasted music I absolutely hated. So, I knew I had to do something to keep us connected.

Because you can't see each other every day, you have to form a strong emotional connection in other ways. Buy a webcam and schedule online "dates." Send each other handwritten letters (doodles of hearts and flowers optional). Decide to read the same books, watch the same movies, or do other activities "together"—like stargazing on the phone with each other. These shared moments will help you to remember that even though he is far away, he is still breathing the same air.

BE THOUGHTFUL

Basically, anything you do to enhance communication in your relationship will help you to feel more connected. Make sure you put thought into every little thing you do. Make him a mix CD of the latest metal songs (even if you detest them!), send him tickets to that concert he mentioned wanting to see, or that basketball game he wanted to watch, etc. Take note of every little thing he says and be creative when it comes to letters, gifts, etc.

KNOW WHAT TO DO WHEN YOU DO SEE EACH OTHER

OK, it's been several weeks or even months since you've seen your significant other. Winter break is around the corner or one of you has decided to visit the other in their new environment. Will it be awkward?

When you first see your partner again, remember that it might be a little different than the last time you saw him. It's a lot easier to notices changes in people we don't see every day than in the ones we do. Some couples will find that they feel the exact same way about each other, and that their partner hasn't changed much since their last visit. Other couples, who sometimes have to spend months apart, can notice big differences the first time they see each other. Be prepared—you never know which situation you will find yourself in! I had been dating my guy for three years before I even left for college, so I figured that as soon as I did see him, of course, everything would go back to normal. Everything was the same for a while—a few months, actually. But as I became less of a presence in his life at home, he started to fill his time with other things, and other people, as did I. I noticed that we related differently—we were both growing up! The distance gave our relationship some renewed excitement.

Also, remember that just like you wouldn't spend every waking moment with your sweetie if he lived close, make sure to give each other some space during visits. You don't get to see each other often, so when you do finally meet up, make the time memorable without suffocating each other.

LET YOUR SWEETIE DO HIS OWN THING

If he comes to visit you and has other friends in the area, encourage him to go out and reconnect with others who are important to him. Just like you'd want to catch up with all your old pals, watch *Gossip Girl*, and drink cheap wine, boyfriends will have their own rituals they want to take part in when they come to visit. If you go to visit him, do the same. Go see some friends or even get up early one morning to grab coffee and explore your beau's new environment. Besides enjoying the opportunity to sleep in, he will appreciate your independence and probably will end up missing you and anxiously waiting for you to return. It's always better to keep him wanting more than for him to feel suffocated by your affection.

DO SOMETHING EXCITING

The best way to keep any relationship exciting is to experience new things together. You should make an effort to split your visit between "down time" with your partner—like lounging on the sofa watching *Nip/Tuck*, nestled in each other's arms—and going out. Even if you simply go out for sushi, attend a lecture on campus, or get drinks at a few bars together, you will have shared a piece of your everyday life with each other and have a new experience together.

MAKE A POINT NOT TO "SURPRISE" EACH OTHER WITH UNPLANNED VISITS

If you live close enough that you could make the trip to see your sweetie on a whim, make sure you clear it with him first. You wouldn't want your beau to intrude on any important plans you may have with your friends, so make sure that you do not do the same. Besides, would you really want to stumble in on a study session that may make you jealous because it happens to be with a few other ladies? Save yourself the drama and call ahead.

ENJOY THE BENEFITS

Don't get me wrong. Long-distance love is difficult, but there are benefits to it as well. Unlike other college couples, who can feel smothered when their lover lives down the hall or in the same apartment complex, long-distance lovers can experience the best of both worlds. Not only can you cultivate your own interests and do your own thing most of the time, you also can enjoy the comfort and satisfaction of being in a committed relationship. You can do all the things you love and you will become a much more interesting person to be with.

ACCEPT CHANGES

The reality is this: people change. This means that the person you started dating six months ago will not be the same person six months from now. In a long-distance relationship this is especially hard to deal with, because you are not around to watch the changes occur. Instead, you might wake up one morning to realize your once super-shy man has turned into a social butterfly. This could come as a major shock, but one important aspect of a long-distance relationship is learning to deal with those feelings and accepting the changes both in yourselves and in your relationship.

FREEDOM OR COMMITMENT: WHICH TO CHOOSE?

If there is one thing that college is universally known for it's freedom. You are finally away from your parents, your boring hometown, and any restricting rules from the past. You don't need to check in with Mom or Dad before going out with the girls, and there is nobody to make sure that you get to bed on time (or go to bed at all!). Relationships, on the other hand, are all about commitment and, yes, restriction. Relationships in college—especially those long distance romances—can seem downright ridiculous to some people. Why shun the very freedom that you've been so longing to have? There is some truth to this assertion. You and your LDR both want to fully enjoy your college lives, but that can seem like a near-impossible task when you're committed to someone halfway across the country. And not every relationship—long-distance or not—is meant to be. So how can you tell if it's time to call it quits?

You have your eye on someone else

This is exactly why long-distance relationships tend not to be satisfying in college. College is the time to explore yourself and your options. You shouldn't feel guilty when you find yourself staring at that cute boy in sociology class with the shaggy hair and Johnny Depp-esque eyes. Being in college gives you an all-access pass to plenty of educated, attractive, and ambitious potential lovers. These lovers can teach you a lot about the world, other people, and even yourself. If you feel even a little inkling that you might want to see other people, it's probably time to wave buh-bye to your cross-country boyfriend and try to connect with someone a little more accessible. As I mentioned earlier, I decided I needed to call it quits with my high school long-distance lover when I started to find myself attracted to a guy in my new group of friends.

Lack of proximity = lack of touch

Any relationship, whether sexual intercourse is involved or not, thrives on the ability to touch one another. Not only is touch essential for humans to develop normally, it is also essential in relationships. Basically, when your lover is hours away, you can't call him up for a late-night cuddle sesh. He can't walk with you hand-in-hand to class, take you out to for a quick bite to eat, and you can't drag him to see the newest Angelina Jolie flick. This lack of physical closeness can put a damper on even the steamiest of relationships. If you find yourself craving a little smooch-fest too often, it may be time to ditch the long-distance romance.

BUT WHY DO WE HAVE TO PART? WE'RE PERFECT TOGETHER

Basically, you think that you and your lover are a match made in heaven. You both adore Kurt Vonnegut, playing the guitar, and don't ever get bored when you're together. So why would you want to part ways with someone who seems perfect for you?

This is an all-too-common problem when deciding to continue a relationship or not. There seems to be no real reason to end the relationship besides the distance factor. Sure, your sweetie resides miles away, but your relationship is peachy. This nonchalance would be fine if you weren't in college—a crucial time for discovering yourself and your interests. Is it really possible that this kind of relationship isn't putting any kind of restriction on you, or hindering your development as an individual in college? Take an honest look at your current situation and you could be surprised. When I was involved in my LDR, I would try to hang out with new friends in my hall, but I'd always be on the phone with, or waiting for a phone call from, my then-boy. I also made frequent trips home, and even though I'd feel left out when the girls would all talk about their weekend plans for frat parties and trips to surrounding cities, I gave that all up for my boy back home. Eventually, my new friends told me that all my "Baby-I-miss-you" phone calls were annoying—and I tried to cut back. But I know now that I'll never get back those adventures I missed out on with those girls—and I can't say I'm happy with my decision to choose a boy over new friends.

So what can you do if you find yourself in a similar situation?

TRY TAKING SOME TIME OFF

Rather than completely ending a seemingly great relationship, try taking a break. Give him—and yourself—some space. Completely cut off communication for a trial period, say a week or so. You will probably be tempted to call your boy, but don't. Do you notice any differences in your relationships with other people? Do you feel more connected to your school—more willing to get involved in activities and spend your time doing things that don't involve waiting for phone calls or planning visits? After the trial period is over, call your BF and discuss how you both felt during your time apart.

But no matter what dating obstacles you encounter during your college years, remember to enjoy every moment and make a conscious decision to learn from each and every one of those stupid mistakes. Really, college is the time to explore who you are, so make sure that your relationship does not restrict this exploration in any way. I cherish the time I spent with my long-distance boyfriend, but we eventually decided to call it quits. I'm happy for that decision—I'm much happier in my current situation. And even though my long-distance relationship was a ton of work, I think, in the end, it was totally worth it…just like all good things in life.

is love possible in an age of hookups?

Jillian E. Sorgini, Hofstra University

e careful with your heart. Sounds a bit cliché, but this is probably the most important lesson that I have learned thus far in my college career. In this new age of hookups, it seems like almost a crime to have any sort of emotional attachment to anyone. The search for love is an idea of the past replaced by the quest of the next hookup—no matter how brief it may be.

Don't get me wrong, a hookup can be extremely satisfying, but only when legitimate feelings aren't involved. Once you find yourself actually liking a person, the desire to detach may lead you to deny the feelings. Ultimately, you are only fooling yourself. I have been the victim of this. What started out as an innocent hookup left me wanting more. For a while I denied it, pretending that I didn't have the time or the effort to put into an actual relationship, but I secretly wanted things to work out. It took its toll. I started to overanalyze everything and even went so far as to blame myself for things not working out. If I could do it over again, I would have paid better attention to my first rule—don't hook up with someone thinking that it will turn into a relationship. The bottom line is that you can't deny your feelings, no matter how good you may be at fooling everyone else.

WHAT EXACTLY IS A HOOKUP?

Before diving any deeper into this important discussion, let's first set the record straight on the exact definition of a hookup. A hookup ranges from kissing to intercourse and anything in between. It can involve multiple partners or one partner, and can be as consistent or inconsistent as you choose. The word "hookup" can refer to the actual person that you hooked up with or the act of hooking up. Other than that, there are no rules involved.

One of my friends says she has many ex-hookups but few ex-boyfriends. Her hookups (we're talking about actual people this time, not just the act), which are always monogamous, last anywhere from 3 months to over a year. If that sounds like something more than a hookup, you're not alone. It qualifies as "boyfriend" to me. But to her and her hookups, they were not comfortable using the term boyfriend or girlfriend. Maybe it signified too much of an emotional commitment. As she would always say when questioned about it, "If something isn't broken, why try to fix it?"

As many of us can attest, it's difficult not to get attached to someone after you are physically intimate with him. After all, your

Did You Know?

So just how many hookups are college girls really having these days?

The jury is still out, but several studies shed a little light on this important question. A 2005 study published in the *Journal of College Health* surveyed undergrads from 4 colleges and found that over 80% of respondents had 1 or fewer sexual partners during the previous year. A 2004 University of Arizona Health and Wellness Survey of their student body found that 73% had 1 or fewer sexual partners. And a Princeton University 2001 study found that 79.3% of respondents had 1 or fewer sexual partners. Far from conclusive, but college women appear to not have as many sexual partners as one might think. It looks like about only 1 in 5 college students has more than 1 sexual partner per year.

brain is wired that way. Touching, hugging, and any other sort of physical contact creates a mental and physical bond with that person. Even if you don't necessarily want a relationship with the person, your body craves that sense of attachment. But here is where the problem lies: when your body is telling you one thing and society tells you another, it's enough to leave anyone confused.

THE STAGES OF A HOOKUP

Like long-term relationships, there are several distinct stages of a typical hookup that may be helpful to know. So, I'll try to explain…

The attraction

Hookups typically don't happen out of the blue. Chances are, if you are hooking up with someone, they have certain alluring qualities that appeal to you. Sometimes it is simply the chase and once you've had your fun, you are done and move on. But sometimes, the hookup can be everything you thought it would be and the thrill of the chase and the unexpected keeps you coming back for more. So you move on to the next stage...

The pseudo-relationship stage

There is a fine line between detachment and attachment. What can start out as an unattached hookup can quickly morph into a pseudo-relationship with real feelings. This is when it gets really confusing. When engaging in any sort of hookup, many of us forget the emotional ramifications.

Is a long-term relationship possible?

Now, I am not saying that all hookups are wrong and always end badly. In some instances, a hookup can turn into something more, but it can take some time. From what I've learned from experience and through friends is that if you gradually ease into hooking up with someone you like, you have more of a chance at having an actual relationship. Easing your way into a hookup gives you and your partner time to establish more than just a physical connection. However, this also means that from the beginning there is some sort of emotional investment before you hook up, so make sure you acknowledge your own feelings and be up-front about them with yourself and your partner.

THE PROBLEM WITH RANDOM HOOKUPS AND YOUR REPUTATION

The truth of the matter is that there is a definite double standard when it comes to hooking up. No one really cares about how many girls a guy has hooked up with. If it's a high number, in fact, he's viewed as a player—not a bad thing. For us girls, the more guys we hook up with, the more negatively we are viewed. It's sad to say, but even in today's society there is still not sexual equality.

However, hooking up can be empowering for a woman. Rather than settling down or being obsessed with finding a boyfriend, the new hookup culture encourages girls to explore their options.

For those women who can hook up and walk away feeling empowered and unattached, all the more power to you. In certain instances, I completely agree with the fact that sometimes a hookup is all you need. Sometimes feelings and emotions can complicate things, and a hookup can be the perfect solution. With the stress of school and other social activities, it can be hard to find time for dating. Sometimes a hookup is a nice release.

SO IS TRUE LOVE POSSIBLE?

As for finding love in this age of the hookup, it is definitely harder—the hookup culture brings a whole new level of complication to the game of love. However, since the rules are yours to make, do what you feel comfortable with doing. If hooking up is not for you, then wait until you meet someone that you care about and prove your friends wrong. Love is out there; you just have to be patient enough to wait for it. While you're waiting, though, never forget the wise words of Janis Joplin: "Don't compromise yourself. You're all you've got."

dormcest: pros and cons

Kristyna Serdock, Stony Brook University

S o you just can't help it. The guy that lives just two doors down from you is just so hot, and you want to get to know him better—a lot better. The dormcest temptation happens to every incoming freshman, because there are so many guys just outside your doorstep day and night. From the occasional hookup to the very serious, engaging in dormcest has its good points and its bad. But you have to play your cards right to avoid as many of these awkward situations as you can (because trust me, they will arise). Weigh this list of pros and cons carefully before getting involved with the boy next door.

PROS

- **He is always around.** If you want to grab some food, need a study buddy, or a study break, you know exactly where to find him.

- **You get to meet his friends from the get-go.** It's always better to get comfortable with his friends early on. That way, you avoid any surprises.

- **You have the perfect way to de-stress when it's time for finals and when all those tough papers are due.** College gets demanding with the finals workload, and now you have a backrub resource at your beck and call.

- **He can look after you.** You never know what can happen on campus, especially with everyone living so close to each other. If a weird situation happens at a party, he'll be sure to keep an eye out for you.

- **You have a reason to stay in.** On busy nights it's so tempting to get pressured into going to all these events after class, but if you don't have the energy after a long day, blame it on him. You have someone to stop by and bug for a bit before you relax for the night.

- **He's your go-to man.** If something comes up unexpectedly and you need a ride or an extra book from the library at 9 o'clock at night, you have someone to turn to. As long as you approach the situation like you're asking for his help and not demanding it, and you're not doing this all too often, he'll understand and help you out.

- **It's the cutest way to start a real relationship.** So many couples I know have gotten together this way. A girl I know met a cute guy down the hall and ended up crashing there one day after class watching TV (episodes of *Lost* and *Grey's Anatomy* seem to work). It's friendly at first, so you start out with this comfort level, which is the most important part of your foundation. Then the TV leads you two to snuggle and you've just moved past friends. Hint: if you have a favorite show in mind that you think he'd be totally into, pick a day every week where you two watch it together. This way you have scheduled hangout time. Just don't go for anything too sappy or serious right away. Pick something fun.

- **Your ego will shoot through the roof.** When you know there's a hot guy you just made out with last night living down the hall, you're going to wake up with the biggest smile on your face.

- **You have the perfect excuse to dress up.** If you know you'll be seeing this guy all the time, then you get a chance to wear all that stuff you'd otherwise end up saving for Friday night. You can also use the whole "dorm room pjs" excuse and walk around in cute boxers and a tee to drive him nuts while you stop by to borrow some DVDs.

CONS

- **They are always around.** If you're not as into the hookup as he is, you're going to be bugged a lot—especially if it's just a physical thing. When a guy knows that someone will give him what he wants, he will try to get it. A lot. It's easy access (I am not calling us easy, but we are just easy to find). If he knows he can walk up the stairs and crawl into your bed, he'll quickly take over your space in an all-consuming way.

- **If you don't like his friends you can't avoid them.** They will always be around his dorm or where he chills. There is no changing that.

- **It can harm your reputation.** There's a 100% chance that other guys know what you and your dorm boy have done together, and once things end with you two (or haven't even ended yet) they might think you do that sort of thing all the time, and will try to get with you as well. However, this sometimes has a strange attraction and positive side to it. If you're cool with it, it's like your relationship résumé is being handed out all over the building.

- **Roommates might not like him or you.** There's always the chance that whoever you're staying with or whoever he's staying with will not like the idea of the two of you always taking up space together. You have to consider their privacy as well, so once this relationship turns into more than just a one-time deal you should have a talk with your roommate to at least let her know where you stand. Maybe you can set up some sort of schedule, or code, but make sure you're not just kicking her out to have some alone time without any warning.

- **The fights will draw a lot of attention.** There are so many people close to your situation who have seen more of your dirty laundry than they should, so when you fight it's probably going to be a spectacle where everyone drops what they're doing and listens in. Bottom line: public fights are embarrassing.

- **If he likes your friend, it'll be obvious.** I'm not sure if this is a better alternative to not knowing or not, but since your relationship is so casual he can openly flirt and you may have to put up with him hitting on your friends. This can be very difficult to watch, since there's a good chance you'll get a front row seat (like at a party or when everyone is hanging in one dorm).

- **If you like someone else, it'll be obvious.** If he's not into seeing other people, or has never tried that before, you could make him uncomfortable if you end up doing that. Keep in mind that there's nothing wrong with this scenario, as long as he knows that you're not being monogamous, but it could still hurt his feelings. You have to be careful with the way you approach this situation, so you know where he's coming from. Otherwise you could end up losing him over someone else even if the other relationship was merely a fling.

- **Someone might want more and the other doesn't.** You might not have been expecting anything serious when you first got involved with this guy, but at some point one of you might start feeling something more. When this happens, handle it as soon as possible. If you're the one who wants more, don't get too clingy. If it happens the other way around, and he's the one who wants to be with you, then you need to be honest and let him down gently.

HOW TO PART WAYS AMICABLY

When things are coming to an end, you should try to do so on friendly terms since you will see them almost every day. Imagine getting the stink eye from this guy at the dining hall, in the community room, and every dorm event for the rest of the year. Yeah, doesn't seem like a lot of fun! For those fearing a miserable ending, here's the no-fail way to get the job done right:

- Get together where you have a minute to talk, but not too long. Plan an event for about half an hour after your conversation starts so you have an excuse to stay on track and bow out gracefully.

- Keep the conversation short and to the point. Plan what you're going to say beforehand so you're not blabbering on to fill up the awkward silences, since there might be a lot of them if this comes out of the blue.

- Once you've said what you needed to say, give him a chance to talk, so he can get his own closure. You owe him that. We've all been dumped out of the blue before, and even if it wasn't a serious relationship it's still confusing when you don't understand why.

- Consider it as though you are helping him learn what not to do in relationships. Answer his questions if he has any, but keep them to the point as well. Be honest or you'll get caught up in lies, and he'll get offended.

- Don't back down if he tries to talk you out of it. You know what you want, so stick to it.

PARTING WORDS

Remember that college is the time for experimentation, so have fun above all else. Treat a fling like a fling and a relationship like a relationship. Keep time for yourself but make sure to share your time with your guy(s) and your friends as well. And never do anything you don't feel comfortable doing, no matter what the circumstances are. Enjoy dorm life for what it is, and you'll have a great time.

U Chic Essentials—Love Life

Focus on you, first

College is the time to focus on *you* first and your love life second. You're going places, and nothing should hold you back from your dreams. If a relationship isn't working out or is even affecting your ability to do your thing, stand strong and make a decision—the relationship either has to change or you have to end it.

Don't fall into the "I Need a Boyfriend Now!" trap

Take your time getting to know yourself before you start stressing about finding someone. It will happen when it's meant to happen, so don't stress yourself out.

Honesty is everything with long-distance love

If your eye is starting to wander and you're trying to maintain a long-distance relationship, don't worry because that's natural. But if you are unhappy or you've taken a serious interest in someone else, then it's time to make up your mind. You'll feel better making a clean, honest break than sneaking around and having to lie.

Looking for more great advice? Head to www.UniversityChic.com and look for "U Chic Picks!" for our fav resources and websites—they come highly recommended from our guide's contributors and editors. Be sure to leave your suggestions as well!

CHAPTER 7

Sorority Chic

*I*s the thought of not knowing many people in college completely stressing you out? Or maybe you're trying to figure out how to get to know more people on campus. The important thing to remember is that you're not alone... pretty much everyone—at some point—is experiencing the same feelings. We've already covered several ways to break the ice and get to know people at your new home. One option we haven't covered in detail—and you're probably curious about!—is sorority membership. Known as "recruitment" or "rush," the formal process of joining a sorority is a great way to get to know a lot of people fast, even if you don't end up committing. From the recruitment process to knowing how to find a sorority that's right for you to dating frat boys to the secrets of sisterhood—everything sorority—we've got you covered!

going greek 101

Donyel L. Griffin, Kean University

I never planned to join a sorority. As soon as I entered Kean University as a curious freshman, a sorority began recruiting me, but I didn't take the bite because it didn't feel like it was for me. I spent my next two years of college without even thinking about Greek life. And then one day I realized I wanted to be more involved in my university, but I wanted something more than joining a club or a group. I suddenly decided that I wanted to go Greek.

Greek Speak

A list of definitions that may come in handy if you are considering Greek membership.

Alumna/Alumnus—Sister or brother of an organization who has graduated.

Big Sister/Big Brother—A member of an organization who guides/directs a new member through and/or after the new-member process.

Bid Day/Bid Night—Is the time where prospective members find out if they will get an invitation to pledge the sorority/fraternity; the process is different for each organization.

Cross—To become an official member of the organization after the initiation process.

Frat Row—A row of fraternity and/or sorority houses located usually near the university.

Greek Alphabet—Refers to the letters Greek organizations use to identify themselves.

Greek Council/Greek Senate—The university system that oversees all Greeks at the university and informs them of news pertaining to Greeks and new policies. Usually there must be a member from each organization who attends meetings on the sorority/fraternity's behalf.

Hazing—Defined as any activities that a group of people makes another person or group of people endure, which may include but is not limited to strenuous activity, embarrassing situations, and anything that a person does not feel comfortable doing but does as a means of "initiation" or "passage."

Interest/Prospective—An individual who demonstrates interest in becoming a member of an organization by attending open events and getting to know members.

Mixer—Refers to a party with a sorority and a fraternity that is closed to anyone but the members of those organizations and sometimes rushees of those organizations.

Paddle—Wooden decorations that usually feature an organization's Greek letters, founding year, symbols, and more. Paddles range from small sizes, for gifts, to large sizes, for display at events.

Pledge—A person going through the process of being a member of their respective organization.

Pledge/Line Sister/Brother—A fellow member who pledges at the same time as you.

Pledging/New Member Education—Term applied for the period of time where you learn the history, traditions, and values of an organization before being initiated as a member.

Recruitment/Rush—Period where interested students have the chance to attend events of an organization in the form of interest meetings, events, and often social outings.

Sisterhood/Brotherhood—The act of behaving as a family of sisters/brothers.

Symbols—A sorority or fraternity's symbol is unique to each organization and has significant meaning to the organization. Often the meaning behind the symbol is kept confidential and known only by the members of that sorority or fraternity.

THE RECRUITMENT PROCESS

Joining a sorority can be beneficial for those who want to become more involved on campus. During my junior year, I was in two classes with a girl who was a member of Lambda Chi Rho, a local sorority founded in 1962 at Kean University. I'd spent my first two years at Kean maintaining a 3.0 GPA for my scholarship while having fun socially, but as my years dwindled down I wanted to get more socially involved. After realizing that not all sororities were obsessed with drinking and partying nonstop (the stereotype we all know) and were actually very diverse, I started attending Lambda Chi Rho recruitment events.

During my rush process, they had open teas or "interest meetings," where we did things like make collages from magazine clippings, throw a Halloween party, make ornaments for a nursing home, and have a mixer with a fraternity. These events helped me see that a sorority could be well-rounded and that I could have fun doing even the simplest things with my potential sisters.

At the end of each interest meeting, the sorority members would ask us recruits if we had any questions about the sorority or Greek life, providing us a platform to express any concerns or raise any questions we had. Having an open forum to ask questions made me feel comfortable about getting involved with my sorority.

FINDING THE RIGHT FIT

Before diving into any formal or informal recruitment process, it's worth putting some thought into what type of sorority you'd like to join. During this process, be sure to seek an organization that focuses on your desires. Do you want a more academic-oriented sorority or one that is more focused on social life? All organizations must maintain a balance among social, academic, and service in order to survive on campus. Some sororities focus on one aspect more than another.

Go to different events of sororities and feel out the girls. Although they, too, will be deciding if you fit, in the end, you want to make sure you like your potential future sisters. It's not enough to join because you know a few people in the house; make sure you can deal with the company of the rest.

FACTORS TO CONSIDER WHEN CHOOSING A SORORITY

How social am I?

You will discover that some sororities have more of a reputation for partying than for hitting the books. Now, of course, not every member will fit these stereotypes. But in most cases, the reputation for the house, overall, proves true...they either meet or exceed their reputation. If you're the honor-roll type and need to go out just once a week to be satisfied, you may find yourself the lone advocate for moderation. And the same goes for the more social gals. Joining an "honor-roll house" may not be the perfect fit for someone needing friends who have an active social calendar.

Perfectionistas?

Some houses aspire to be at the top of everything: top grades, top number of charity hours, top intramural teams, top awards at the annual Greek Award ceremony (almost every university has these), etc. If you're the perfectionist type, then these houses are probably a good fit for you. Just remember that you may be asked to commit a little more time than usual to sorority activities, and the expectations on you may be higher.

Are all the members from the same high school or city?

It's not unusual for a particular sorority to have several members from the same city or high school—friends recruit friends. If you are in the minority—let's say that you're from a public school in Chicago while the rest of the house is from a top private school in St. Louis—you may feel a little out of the loop. But it all depends. A go-with-the-flow personality will have no trouble fitting in while others may be happier with a little more diversity.

A popular house?

If you're leaning toward membership in a particular house for no other apparent reason than it's known for being a good one at your school, fugettaboutit! There is no such thing as a good vs. bad house. A sorority will be "good" as long as it's a good fit for you. Focus first on where you feel most comfortable (after all, you'll be spending a lot of time with these ladies) because if you're paying attention during the recruitment process, you'll know it. That way, you'll be less likely to be taken with the "popularity factor" when making this important decision.

Bottom line: if you want to join a sorority, do so for the right reasons—*your* reasons. Don't join something because it sounds good or your friends think you should do so. If you don't follow your gut instinct, you'll end up unhappy with your decision, maybe even dropping out. Don't let this be you. There is almost always a place for everyone who wants to join.

HOW TO JOIN

Organizations vary in requirements for membership, but usually you must take part in a recruitment process or "rush" first, which consists of events organized by the sorority to help you get to know them better and vice versa. Each college and university has a timetable for the official recruitment process. Check your school's website or Greek life directory to get this information. Also, be aware that some chapters have an informal process as well that occurs at a different time of the year.

The formal recruitment process

Formal recruitment is different at every school and in some cases every sorority. Some schools have a week set aside—sometimes before school begins in the fall—where all Greeks get to recruit new members. Other schools may extend the process over a two-to three-week time period. Large universities will require everyone that is interested in joining a fraternity or sorority to sign up with the interfraternity council at the university. Once the recruitment process begins, each potential recruit is required to visit every sorority at least once to talk to them and find out what they're about. Schools require this in order to make the process more fair; the hope is that by seeing each sorority and witnessing the diversity among the houses, you, as a potential recruit, will choose a house based on personal preferences rather than joining a house because someone told you to.

As for what to expect each day during the process, you will attend multiple events while you are narrowing down your list of sororities that you're interested in joining. Remember that sororities will be doing the same thing to you. You will then revisit the houses where there is mutual interest. You may not get an invitation back to a particular house. If this happens to you, do not take this as a rejection and get down about it. They're not rejecting "you"; they don't even know you. There is a lot of randomness to the process, and the decision to invite someone back is often based on factors out of your control—sororities may give preferences to girls simply because they know someone in the house or come from a particular high school. And then there are the preferences that go to "legacies." A legacy in a sorority is a woman whose mother, aunt, sister, or sometimes grandmother was a member of a sorority, and this increases the chances of a girl getting a bid to pledge. All organizations do not accept the concept of a legacy, but most do. Formal recruitment ends when bids are given out.

The informal recruitment process

Unlike the formal recruitment process, which is typically organized by the university, informal recruitment happens when you befriend members of a sorority outside of the formal period of recruitment. Usually, girls going through informal recruitment were interested in a sorority but did not have the time to pledge that semester, or changed their mind on membership and have expressed an interest in Greek life.

My "Informal" Greek Experience

Kara Apel, University of South Carolina

When I got my Greek Life brochure in the mail the summer before my freshman year, I barely glanced at it for more than five minutes. All I could see was fake. Fake hair. Fake tans. Fake smiles. "Fake" was definitely a word I thought described sororities to a tee.

But even without this negative impression, "rushing" in the fall would have been really hard for me to do. I was lucky to have made the Carolina Coquettes (the University of South Carolina's football dance team) for my freshman year. Sorority rush week was the same week as "hell week" for Coquettes, when we had three practices each day. Even if I had wanted to go through the sorority recruitment process, it would have been practically impossible to do. With this in mind, I closed my brochure and basically closed my mind to joining a sorority.

The summer flew by, and the start of school came, along with rush. That first week of school, I watched the girls on my dorm floor running around like chickens with their heads cut off trying to figure out what to wear for each day of the recruitment process. As I watched them do this, I couldn't help but wonder why these girls would put themselves through all this stress during an already stressful first week of school. However, as the semester crept by, I started to understand why. The sorority girls that lived in my dorm were constantly going to mixers, participating in Greek-life events, and having a blast hanging out with their "sisters." I had already made friends on my own without the help of a sorority, but somehow I couldn't help but feel like I was missing out on what seemed to be a fun aspect of college life. Surprisingly enough, I was starting to become a little jealous of the girls that I had brushed aside as fake earlier in the year. In the end, I decided to go through informal rush that next spring semester, and ended up pledging Gamma Phi Beta, a national sorority. I am so glad that I gave sorority life a second chance.

My journey to becoming a member of a sorority was not the normal ride. Not everyone gets the luxury of rushing in the spring, but if you can, I would definitely recommend it. Looking back, I'm glad I didn't rush my first semester in college because it really allowed to me to settle in and figure out who I was before I joined a sorority.

Typically if you are hanging out with members of a sorority—like going to the movies or hanging out at their house—you are participating in the informal recruitment process. There are no time constraints on informal recruitment. The goal with informal recruitment is simply to provide another opportunity for girls who did not participate in formal recruitment, whatever the reason.

U Chic Tip!

Be careful about looking like you're "shopping" too much for the right sorority. Sometimes your indecisiveness, if witnessed by members of a house that you've expressed interest in, can make them second-guess your true interest in their sorority and may affect your chances of getting a bid from them later.

WORK ANY LEGACY TIES YOU HAVE

If you have a family member who is an alumna of a sorority that has a chapter at the school you're attending, call them up! Usually she will still be involved or have connections with her sorority and can give you more details on what it is like to be a member. Also, she may be able to help you through the rush process by sending a letter to the chapter on your behalf in advance of the process. Many sororities will take alumnae connections (especially if your mom belonged) into consideration when making bids to potential future members of their chapter. If you don't have these legacy ties, no worries. These ties will not make or break your chance to be a member of a particular house, since there are usually only a few members a year at most who are legacies.

PLEDGING

After rush, the members of the sorority that you've expressed an interest in will decide whether they believe you would fit in as a member. If their decision is yes, they will extend an invitation or bid to join. It is then up to you to decide which sorority or house fits you best, and then accept one of the offers of membership.

Once you accept a bid, there will be a new member education process, also known as pledging. Pledging differs from organization to organization, and unfortunately some sororities and fraternities have taken the pledging process to a negative extreme by occasionally making the news for hazing, although today there are much fewer bad incidents than in the past. That's why you might want to be on the lookout during recruitment for each house's pledging process to make sure that it's worth the time and commitment in order to become a member.

BECOMING A SISTER

It can get frustrating going through the pledge process since it can go on for several weeks, and may take some of your time away from school. Annoyances aside, pledging is important because it bonds you with the other women who are in your pledge class, helping you learn the values, history, and traditions of the sorority. I had two pledge sisters whom I became very close with during the process and they are still good friends today. A pledge sister or brother is the term used most often for mainstream sororities and fraternities, while traditionally African American, Hispanic, and multicultural organizations refer to the people they go through the process with as a "line sister" or "line brother."

Many sororities have a more educational approach to pledging than making you do silly or harmful things. When I pledged my sorority, there was a lot of tradition, history, and education that I had to learn during the pledging process. I was never forced to drink, walk around in the woods blindfolded, or do anything else that caused me mental or physical harm. And you, too, should be able to have the same positive experience. If not, then it's time to say something to the house leadership or even taking your complaint to school administrators. In some cases, you may have to speak up for a friend who is being mistreated. Also don't be afraid to drop out of a house that is involved in hazing. No one should have to put up with mistreatment of any kind in order to join any organization.

Finally, don't let the uncertainties of the entire recruitment and pledging process prevent you from considering sorority membership. Remember, everyone else is in the same boat. Until you are a member you will not be able to completely understand the entire system and truly appreciate it for what it is.

Don't be afraid to drop out of a house that is involved in hazing. No one should have to put up

with mistreatment of any kind in order to join
any organization.

MONEY, MONEY, MONEY!
So, are you really just paying for friends?

For years one of my friends would say that she'd never join a sorority because she wouldn't "pay for friends." Back then, I agreed with her, although I never put down any of my roommates or acquaintances who were in a sorority. However, after joining, I came to realize that the money you pay is not "for friends" but for financial expenses the sorority will incur for the year.

Where does the money go?

Sororities have a treasury and treasurer (who is usually on the executive board) who oversees finances. Money from the treasury is usually applied to fund-raisers, recruitment events and T-shirts, "Meet the Greeks"-type campus activities, or other important events. Also, chapters of national sororities pay dues to their national headquarters. National organizations have hundreds of chapters nation- and worldwide, and are basically run like a business at the headquarters level.

Other expenses you can expect

Budgeting is very important to maintaining a sorority membership. My sorority has payment plans for girls who cannot afford the dues in total, as we all understand that other school expenses can make it difficult to pay at times.

In fact, sometimes we will even pay for another sister's dues when they cannot afford it for whatever reason, because, after all, we are a sisterhood and really do feel like family.

> Budgeting is very important in maintaining a sorority membership. My sorority has payment plans for girls who cannot afford the dues in total, as we all understand that other school expenses can make it difficult to pay at times.

LIVING ARRANGEMENTS

Many of you may have heard of sorority houses. A sorority or fraternity house is the house of the organization and is usually located somewhere near the university. Some of these houses are merely for meetings and administrative purposes; other houses are actual homes where members are expected to live at some point in their college careers (usually sophomore and junior year). Some houses can only hold 20 members while some go up to 100! At big colleges and universities, recruitment events and bid day are held at the sorority house. However, some schools don't have sorority houses, so the members will instead take up a couple of floors in a dormitory building or apartment complex. The reason for the closeness is because members benefit when they can interact with one another on issues pertaining to the sorority and have meetings and access to one another.

Keep in mind that just because you've joined a sorority does not mean that you have to live in the same house or floor as your sisters. Usually, you will have options for where you live. At most larger universities you will live in a sorority house near campus with 50–100 other girls during your sophomore and junior years, but you will have options for where you live during your freshman and senior years. At my college, there isn't a frat row (an area typical of some colleges where the entire street is lined with sorority and fraternity houses) or an area specifically for Greek housing. However, I know many members of different Greek organizations who have rented or bought their own houses around the college, and it serves as their unofficial "house."

FINAL WORD

So after it's all said and done, is a sorority for you? Even if you're not sure about it but are still curious, go through the recruitment process to try it out. And don't feel pressured to rush a sorority when you first arrive on campus. You're in college to learn, grow, and explore. If joining a sorority is an important part of the collegiate experience for you, then great! If not, then great as well! Seize the moment when you feel it is right. If you don't meet the sorority of your dreams your freshman year, you may discover it later on in college like I did. Best advice I can give: always keep your options open.

life as a greek

Donyel L. Griffin, Kean University

As an incoming college student, you probably have had minimal to no experience with sororities, and maybe wondering what they exactly do. Is there anything more to it than partying? Yep. Here's a quick summary.

CHARITABLE PURPOSES

Charity is a big part of any Greek organization, and for my organization, certain events are mandatory. It doesn't mean you get scolded if you cannot attend an event. These events are something we recognize as important to the survival and mission of the sorority. First, you'll most likely be expected to attend community service events. Usually, the sorority will host a philanthropic event like a walk or run, while some events are sponsored by the college. At my school, for example, the Kean University Greek Senate hosts the "Somerset Hills Holiday Party," where we do crafts with kids from a school. The senate also hosts "Up Til Dawn," which raises money for St. Jude's Children's Hospital. All Kean University organizations are required to have representatives attend these events whether it's the entire organization or just two people. A lot of Greeks always show up to these events. And why not? They're fun!

SOCIAL TIME

You've probably been curious about the social aspect. Being in a sorority does encourage you to be social not only within your own house but with other Greeks and students at your university as well.

Most sororities have "mixers" with fraternities, which are parties exclusively for that sorority and fraternity. Mixers are usually big events, and for the most part, you'll probably be expected to go (especially those during the recruitment season). In addition to these mixers and meetings, there are other functions as well, like sisterhood outings, cocktail parties, and formals that bring back memories of high school prom. For the most part, these events are not mandatory.

Most colleges have Greek Week to encourage unity among Greeks with events, outings, games, and on-campus activities. At my school, our version is Greek Olympics. During Greek Olympics, organizations compete against one another for points in events like softball, pool, basketball, tug of war, volleyball, and dodgeball. My sorority ended up winning third place. It's not all about winning but it did feel good for us to get a Greek Olympics trophy for one of the first times in recent years!

THE FRATS

As previously mentioned, there will be several opportunities to "mix" with fraternity guys either through parties or some type of cohosted charity event. Some houses may even have a brother/sister relationship with one another where they "mix" often, team up for service projects, and support one another with recruitment and pledging.

As for the dating scene, as a Greek I've never dated a fraternity guy so cannot speak from personal experience, but I have plenty of friends or sorority sisters who have. Based on what I've heard about my friends' experiences, there are some definite pros and cons to dating a fraternity guy.

If you're dating a guy from a particular fraternity, this gives you an opportunity to set some of your single sisters up with his brothers. Also, you will both understand where each other is coming from in terms of what it means to be a Greek member. Some non-Greeks don't understand the reasoning behind all the weekly meetings and events, making it hard to have a relationship during the busy times.

Sometimes dating a frat guy can be overkill on Greek life when Greek-related stuff is all you ever seem to talk about. Another con is no matter how close your sorority is with your boyfriend's fraternity, keep in mind that they will have to mingle and sometimes network with other sororities. For some girls, this may be difficult as jealousy sometimes comes into play. You might want to also think about the future. For example, if you break up with the guy, what happens? As one sorority sister put it, "It can be as simple as a hookup with a guy from a fraternity to make it feel weird to mix or hang out with the entire fraternity."

Many girls feel like dating a frat guy goes hand in hand with being in a sorority, but it doesn't. If it works for you, great! But don't feel pressured to date or hook up with a frat guy if you think it's not for you or may cause problems in the long run.

GPA AND OTHER REQUIREMENTS

Other sorority responsibilities include weekly chapter meetings and having to keep up certain grade requirements. Yes, surprise! Most sororities do have grade requirements for their members. Your Greek system may have a minimum GPA of 2.3 or more to join a house! Some houses may even consider your high school record when deciding to offer an invitation for membership. It makes sense: students who can't obtain satisfactory grades usually won't be able to balance the requirements of belonging to a Greek organization with their school activities. If your grades do meet the requirements to join, but for some reason you fall behind after pledging, your chapter may require that you complete a certain number of study hours per week. But every campus and house is different. It all depends. Most sororities have required weekly meetings to discuss upcoming events, fund-raisers, new ideas, or other important issues. These meetings are ones that cannot be missed.

A Lifelong Commitment

Miryam Chico, a sister of the International Latina sorority Gamma Phi Omega, Kean University

I believe my sorority's motto truly encompasses what sisterhood means to me: "Unity and Sisterhood, Now and Forever, One and Inseparable." A sisterhood is a lifelong commitment and experience. It doesn't end when you graduate college. It's something you work at throughout your life, and gain immeasurable memories and relationships from. Sisterhood has allowed me to not only learn about a different group of women, but also to grow and learn from them. I've gained lifelong friendships that I would not have found elsewhere. Sisterhood has provided me with a network of people who share my joys and sorrows, and also act as a source of encouragement and support, especially as an undergraduate since I was an out-of-state student who didn't know anyone on my campus.

Besides the mandatory activities, it's entirely up to you how involved you want to be in your sorority. Some members are highly active while others may be less active for personal or financial reasons. When I first joined my sorority, I never imagined that I'd become vice president, later president, and then chosen as Greek Senate Sorority Sister of the Year! It all depends on how much you want to be involved and—like everything in life—your sorority experience will be what you make of it.

SISTERS FOREVER

Being in a sorority is not like joining the softball team or choir or student government. While all of those activities are great, your strong attachment to them usually ends once you graduate college. Whereas, in a sorority, you're a sister forever, long after your responsibilities as a student ends.

The bond forms as soon as you join

Many sororities and fraternities adopt the terms "big sister" and "little sister," or in my sorority we refer to it as just "big" and "little." And while the process for choosing little sisters differs from organization to organization, it has the same goal: ensuring that someone is there to guide a new member into the organization and beyond. In my house, everyone has a "big" that picked them when they were "little." And then once you are eligible for a "little," it's your turn to start the process again.

No matter what terminology you use, when picking a "little," you want someone you think you will get along with or have something in common. When I picked my little I liked that she was very motivated academically and she seemed to have an easygoing personality while being strong-minded. With time and a little effort, many big/little relationships have transcended college. Of course, not all big/little relationships will be close, but for many they are. In fact, for some girls, it's like having the older or younger sister they never had.

Networking beyond college

Many girls benefit from alumni interaction. Even in a local sorority like mine, networking is extremely important. One of my alumni sisters was able to get an internship at a magazine, and later a job, through an affiliation with another alumni sister who worked at Time, Inc. Although, alumni move on and develop careers and families and other obligations throughout life, a part of them feels a sense of loyalty to the sorority and even to sisters they may have never met. This most likely will be the same case for your sorority. So, don't hesitate to reach out to those who have come before you. They are there to lend a hand.

For me, sisterhood means a support system, a family away from home, and a group of girls who share common goals. Everyone is not the same and never will be, and in any organization, you are bound to be closer with some more than others. But if you stick it out through the good and the bad, your dedication will most likely result in an experience that will provide benefits to you throughout your lifetime.

U Chic Essentials—Sorority Chic

Forget the stereotypes

Leave the stereotypes at the door. Within each sorority, you'll find a diverse group of women from a variety of backgrounds and with different interests. Really, there is no such thing as a cookie-cutter sorority.

Consider informal recruitment for a less-intense process

Informal recruitment is a great option, as it lasts a little longer, is more casual, and provides you a better opportunity to have more one-on-one time with the sorority members of a prospective house. However, as sororities use informal recruitment to fill their quotas, not all sororities will offer an informal process, one of the main differences from formal recruitment.

Greek life is not for everyone

If after speaking with friends who are sorority members or even going through recruitment you still are questioning whether you should join a house, it may not be the right thing for you. And guess what: that's OK! There are *plenty* of other things for you to get involved with in college.

Looking for more great advice? Head to www.UniversityChic.com and look for "U Chic Picks!" for our fav resources and websites—they come highly recommended from our guide's contributors and editors. Be sure to leave your suggestions as well!

CHAPTER 8

Healthy and Happy

idterms, papers, friendships, boyfriends, all-nighters, pub crawls. All of these activities and interactions—some more fun than others—can take a toll on your health in college. And it probably comes as no surprise that your health and happiness are important components of the fabulous college life. This chapter covers health issues you may face in college, but is by no means comprehensive. To completely be up to speed on all health matters, visit your school's student health center or their website for a more complete picture. But to get you started, we've tackled the common issues and concerns that you may face, giving you a crash course on staying healthy and happy in college.

dealing with the blues

Janine Camara, University of North Carolina—Greensboro

Leaving behind nights of terror and fear, I rise, into a daybreak that's wondrously clear, I rise.
—Maya Angelou, "Still I Rise"

*Y*our dorm room has become a refuge where you retreat from feelings of doubt, anger, and hopelessness. You can't remember the last time you had enough energy to make it to a coffee date with your friends or your weekly art class at the YMCA. And most of all, there's a lingering haze of despair that seems to follow you everywhere. You've tried to push it aside hoping it would dissolve in the midst of homework, club meetings, and finals, but it hasn't. And now you're at your wit's end. It's starting to take a toll on your productivity and you're not eating well, or hardly eating at all. If this scenario paints a reality that is all too similar to your own, *stop*. Understand that what you're going through isn't just a bout of homesickness or the blues. You may be dealing with depression.

THE BLUES OR SOMETHING ELSE

We all face periods of sadness. From the "winter blues," which can be caused by a lack of sunshine during the winter, to a period of sadness after a breakup with a boyfriend, it's common to have times when you just don't feel like your normal, more positive self. But these moments usually last for no more than a few weeks or even a month or two.

So how do you know if it's merely a fleeting case of the blues or something more serious? Feeling blue poses a serious problem when your sad feelings linger, according to Dr. Kala Annambhotla, staff psychologist of the Counseling and Testing Center at the University of North Carolina–Greensboro.

"It's normal for people to feel sad, anxious, or discouraged from time to time," Annambhotla said. "These feelings usually lift within a few days to a week, as people find solutions and support from friends," she continued. "Students should seek professional help when they notice that their low mood lasts too long or occurs frequently, when symptoms feel severe, when they notice that their mood is causing academic, social, or other problems, and/or when they feel stuck and can't seem to solve the problems causing the depression."

If your feelings do not subside and they are starting to affect your work and everyday life, you may be suffering from clinical depression and should consider seeking professional help. Now, before you start freaking out that there is something horribly wrong with you, take heart! Though it may seem as though you're alone in your struggle with a depressed mood and constant sadness, you're not. According to HalfofUs.com, an online portal for college students coping with mental health issues, "nearly half of all college students reported feeling so depressed that they couldn't function during the last school year." That's a lot of people!

Even more surprising is a World Health Organization (WHO) statistic that depression affects 121 million people around the world. According to the website of the nonprofit medical practice Mayo Clinic, depression can manifest itself in a variety of forms, ranging from "mild" to "severe." Mayo Clinic describes clinical depression as being a "severe persistent form of depression."

Common causes of depression

The stresses of college, if unmanaged, can lead to depression. Take Maria Pascucci for example. Her self-imposed pressure to succeed led to high levels of stress and ultimately depression during high school and college.

"My biggest stressors during college were balancing academics with outside employment and a constant worry about the future. Uncertainty about the future scared me to death, and not living up to the high expectations I'd placed on myself," Pascucci said. The pressure to succeed raised her stress quotient and took a toll on her well-being. "I was battling stomachaches, insomnia, and depression. During my last semester of my senior year, I had a panic attack after finding myself unprepared for a final exam in Women's History and bolted out of the classroom," Pascucci said.

For Pascucci, counseling and yoga were vehicles that helped propel her toward recovery. She recounts her story below in an excerpt from the article "New Year's Resolutions: Love, Me."

> For a while I wallowed in self-pity. Then I was simply tired of being angry and chose to move on. I started working through my rigid expectations through journaling and with the help of a counselor. We talked about how I was really failing no one but myself by never trying new things for fear of making mistakes. My counselor suggested that I try yoga to soothe my anxiety. She said that I needed to practice mindfulness. I shrugged my shoulders and said, "Whatever, my mind is working *all* the time." What my counselor meant was that I was spending so much time always thinking that I never stopped to look around and appreciate what was right in front of me.

Now Pascucci is the president and founder of CampusCalm. com and CampusCalmU.com, a Web portal and company dedicated to helping students deal with the stresses of high school and college life. She is proof that depression is an obstacle that can be overcome.

HOW TO BEAT IT

Your depression may seem like an impossible obstacle to get around. But like all things in life, there is definitely a light at the end of the tunnel. Statistics say that most people respond positively to treatment. WHO reports that treatment such as psychotherapy and antidepressant medication proved to be helpful for between 60% to 80% of people suffering from depression.

Talk with loved ones

As the nonprofit group Mental Health America notes, depression can happen to anyone, at any age, at any time, so you shouldn't get down on yourself for feeling the way you do. Depression isn't something you should keep hidden or feel ashamed of. The best way to deal is to be open about what you're going through, like Maria Pascucci who, for example, opened up to a counselor about her feelings.

Annambhotla's advice to depressed students echoes Pascucci's story: "I advise depressed students to talk with supportive friends and professionals and be patient with themselves as they recover. They may want to simplify their life while still pursuing goals that are important to them. Learning to accept yourself and taking pride in your accomplishments is so important."

Quit being so hard on yourself

Annambhotla also said that antidepressant medication may also be an option for students who are experiencing decreased levels of energy and disrupted eating and sleeping patterns. By taking the steps to get the help you need, you can help put yourself on the road to recovery and the reclaiming of your sense of self-worth.

TOOLS FOR DEALING WITH DEPRESSION

Your Campus Health Center—Your campus health center is staffed with knowledgeable and understanding professionals who have experience helping students deal with depression. You can call ahead to make your appointment and stop over on your way to bio lab.

HalfofUs.com—A website dedicated to helping college students deal with a range of mental and emotional health issues, touching on topics like depression, cutting, and drug and alcohol abuse. The website includes information about depression, testimonials from celebrities and college students about their struggles with depression, and an online assessment called "Check Yourself," that allows you to screen yourself or a friend for a mental health disorder.

CampusCalm.com—This website is geared toward college and high school students and offers tips and articles for dealing with academics, self-esteem, and self-worth. The site offers a free online "Stress Less" kit, and has other valuable information.

MayoClinic.com—The website of this nonprofit medical practice has detailed information on depression. It outlines the signs and symptoms to look for, the possible causes of depression, and the different methods for treating depression.

sex ed 101

Aja Johnson, University of Maryland– College Park

hile many of you will be signing up for calculus or political science, there doesn't seem to be many open sections for talk about the birds and bees. When I told my friend I was writing this section, she laughed, "What's there to know about sex? Use a condom and get in there!" But that's the problem! Everyone assumes they know everything they already need to know about sex, and if not, they always have their latest issue of *Cosmo*.

Although you may think you're the sex guru, even you can benefit from a no-nonsense guide on sex in college to keep all the facts straight. Now, by no means do I purport to be the definitive expert in this field. Heck, people spend years in medical school and residency learning about the more complicated aspects surrounding sex. But thanks to several years in college and having to face the variety of sex-related issues that can come up, I have some real-world advice that can help you prepare. So sit down, strap in, and get your number two pencils ready, for you have just enrolled in Sex Ed 101.

FOR THE FIRST-TIMERS

Breathe. Having sex is not as daunting as it seems. First, you must realize what your own expectations are about sex. Even if this isn't your first trip to the rodeo, your feelings toward sex can fluctuate and it's important to be honest about your expectations. These expectations can be physical (*to the left, no right, yeah that's it*) or they can be emotional (*not yet...let's wait...OK, NOW, NOW, NOW I'm Ready!*). Each sexual experience you have may not be the same—even if you're doing it with the same partner! So while that McDreamy fantasy is great to keep on standby, don't freak out if it doesn't happen your first time.

Once you've made the decision that you're ready to have sex, it's best to schedule an appointment with your gynecologist just so you know what you're working with. Your doctor can also talk to you about pregnancy and diseases. This includes prevention and detection. The only surefire way to prevent pregnancy or disease is via abstinence. There are also other options you can consider to limit the risks. There's birth control, which if used properly, is over 99% effective in preventing pregnancy. Birth control can come in the form of a pill, shot, or an external device being implanted in your body. It's best to talk to your doctor about these options and what may be the best one for you.

If you've already had sex and haven't seen a doctor, you should get yourself checked out. Sex can breed a bunch of baddies that, if ignored, can become a big nasty problem. If you don't have your own doctor, talk to your general practitioner and see if they have any information on how to find a gynecologist. You can also check out your health center on campus to see if they have a women's health services center. My school has a full-service women's health department (with on-call gynecologists). If they can't do it in-house, they'll be able to direct you to the proper place that can.

> While a friend is a great resource, it's better to discuss these matters with a physician. It's like cutting your hair—would you trust your best bud or your stylist with a pair of scissors? Think of it that way, but with your vagina, which is a tad more important than a new do.

When you're in your doctor's office, feel free to ask questions, questions, and more questions! Talk about discharge! Talk about pain! If something seems off, bring it up. Don't feel embarrassed; they've heard it all. Your sexual health is one of the most important things to protect. Being uneducated can lead to risky behavior, resulting in problems that you'll have to deal with for the rest of your life. This is the time you can address STIs (sexually transmitted infections), vaccines, birth control, even a change of diet or ask about that thing you saw on TV (*can I really twist my body like that?*). In addition to any health concerns, this is also a great place to learn about your body and libido. While a friend is a great resource, it's better to discuss these matters with a physician. It's like cutting your hair—would you trust your best bud or your stylist with a pair of scissors? Think of it that way, but with your vagina, which is a tad more important than a new do.

HOW TO PROTECT YOURSELF

As previously mentioned, the surefire way to protect yourself is through abstinence. The next best way to prevent diseases is to use the barrier method. What I'm referring to here is the use of condoms when engaging in both vaginal and anal intercourse. There are different types of condoms, which include male condoms that create a barrier around the penis and female condoms that create a barrier inside the vagina. It's best to try different condoms and brands to see what works best for you. Latex is most popular (they prevent pregnancy about 97% of the time if used properly), but for those with an aversion to latex, try polyurethane condoms. (All other condoms—sheepskin, lambskin, etc.—don't perform as well, and you will be doing yourself a disservice by playing with them.) Condoms also come in a variety of sizes, and while there are XXLs, believe me when I say it's all fluff. If you've sat in a sexual-health presentation, you may remember the part when they stretch the condom over their forearm. Snag a free condom from your health center, and try it out yourself.

Condoms can serve as a barrier when performing oral sex on a male. There are even flavored and specialty condoms, for more flair. When performing oral sex on a female, it's best to use a dental dam. Dental dams stretch across the vulva, and create a barrier between the mouth and genitals to prevent disease. Most dental dams can be found via sexual health centers, or at special sex shops. Unfortunately, some infections spread to areas not covered by condoms. Therefore it's best to talk to your partner about their sexual history.

WHAT TO DO WHEN YOUR PROTECTION FAILS

Now that you know how to protect yourself if things go right, what do you do if things go wrong? Although condoms are a medically proven method of protection, there are times when they could slip off, break, or even get stuck inside your vagina. While these things don't happen often, it's important to be careful and make sure you're using it the right way, as incorrect usage leads to faulty results. When using condoms, always make sure you leave space at the tip to allow for shifting during ejaculation. Also, always check the expiration date, as expired condoms can be more brittle and ineffective.

So what do you do when your protection fails? Don't freak! You can engage in a backup method, such as emergency contraception. Emergency contraception pills (Plan B is approved for use in the United States) contain a heightened dose of progestin that acts almost like a supercharged birth control pill. Just as the label says, it should only be used in an emergency, and is only effective up to 120 hours after sex. So it would be best to take it as soon as possible. Remember, it is not 100% effective against pregnancy, and is not at all effective against STIs. It would also be best to get yourself checked out by a doctor, because it has happened that remnants of the condom are left inside.

PREGNANCY & STIS

The best way to find out if you're pregnant is to track your cycle and mark it in a place that you regularly update, like your planner. Once you notice your period is out of whack, make an appointment with your doctor for a follow-up and grab an over-the-counter pregnancy test while you're waiting for the appointment. But it's important to not solely rely on these tests as they can end up being wrong.

Detection for STIs is a little more difficult than just looking at your calendar, especially since most STIs show little to no symptoms. Regular checkups with your doctor will help detect STIs. When you're being examined, make sure that they are testing you for *everything*—that includes the standard group of STIs, including herpes and HPV. In between checkups, do your own inspection. Prop yourself up in your bathroom, prep yourself with a mirror, and make sure that there is good lighting. Don't worry about feeling silly. It's yours—why not check out the goods?

If something feels or looks wrong, check in with your doctor. If it's nothing, mazel tov. It's just best to be sure. If you do find out that you have an STI, make sure you talk to your partner(s) and tell them to get tested. Awkward, of course, but it has to be done. Otherwise, they can't protect themselves or others.

> Don't worry about feeling silly.
> It's yours—why not check out the goods?

TAKE ADVANTAGE OF THE RESOURCES AROUND YOU

No matter what situation you're facing sexually, there are a *ton* of resources on campus. Some schools may offer more services on campus than others, but most provide students with the information they need. Your best bet is to look to your campus health center. These centers are such a huge resource because they cater specifically to the college demographic. As a result, they focus on issues that impact college kids the most, such as pregnancy, STIs, and diseases that may begin to show up in a young adult. They offer all sorts of resources, and usually provide pamphlets, health guides, free condoms, and peer-education programming.

If you find that your health center on campus does not carry information on sexual health, there are still other resources you can try. First, ask your health coordinator if they work with any particular hospitals or clinics in the area. If they don't have any ties to any local centers, hit the Web and look for local hospitals and health centers. Or go to your local government's resource page, or nationally recognized organizations, such as Planned Parenthood. There's plenty of information out there—you just have to find it!

CHOOSING ABSTINENCE

Before we end this class, it's worth mentioning abstinence. When it comes to sex, the first question you must address is whether or not you plan to have sex in the first place. Since sex is such an individualized experience you need to make sure that you're having it or not having it for the right reasons. It may be helpful to weigh out your feelings and see how that corresponds with your values, beliefs, and your life plan. If you find that remaining abstinent is important to you, choose it and embrace it. While the decision to abstain is a personal one, sometimes it becomes difficult when you're surrounded by people who may not relate to you and your decision. But just because they may not share the same ideas doesn't mean that they won't understand. So, don't be afraid to stand your ground in a challenging discussion or situation.

Most times, your friends will be supportive, but intimate relationships are a whole other matter. What's most important is to be up-front about your needs with your partner, and to express your desire to abstain. Sure, there might be some jerks out there who will tease you or even get angry or pushy; don't back down. But by and large, if you're honest and up-front with your partner from the beginning, they'll understand that it's a decision that's important to you and will respect you for it.

And don't forget that there are many other ways to be intimate without having sex. Touching and kissing can be just as intense as going all the way. Also, don't underestimate the power of words. Some couples I know who practice abstinence undergo these intense dream sequences where they describe their sexual fantasies in a safe and personal environment. This creates a feeling of physical intimacy without actually having to be physical.

There's so much to say about safe sex that there are not enough pages in this book to cover it, but I hope this crash course has provided a good overview for all you potential sex goddesses out there.

a self-confidence boost

Aja Johnson, University of Maryland–College Park

When I first went away to school, it was like an experience I could have dreamed up. It was four hours away from my old stomping grounds, and my first time away from home. As a girl with such a strong social circle, it was weird being light-years away from everything that was familiar to me. Don't get me wrong; I was no wallflower. I was busy buzzing around campus, meeting new people, staying out late, getting in trouble, and doing all of the great things that could only go on in a college setting (where else can you get delivered fresh brownies at the drop of a dime, or partake in a midnight round of freeze tag?). Though, between the food and the fun, I noticed something missing. While I was doing things that were fun, new, and exciting, there was a part of me that felt I was drifting into the background…that somehow my self-confidence was losing out.

One of the best things about college life is the ability to get caught up in anything. It's spontaneous, it's crazy, and can be completely out of your element and comfort zone. Although fun, it can also be a bad thing for your self-confidence.

A CULTURE SHOCK

As I drifted from party to party, running into girls from my hall and guys from my classes, I found myself bending to complement each situation. I was paranoid that I wasn't smart, pretty, or cool enough. I thought I was talking too much, saying too little, and was afraid they would find out about me. I was afraid they would know I was cheating, applying a smile with each swipe of my lip gloss. I wasn't being fake, but I was stretched too thin. I began blending into the background and found myself not knowing who I was anymore.

Over time this tore at me, since I didn't realize what was happening. The littlest things bought me down; I overanalyzed, and because of it, my self-confidence all but disappeared. I began doubting myself and my individual shine became lackluster. How could this happen to the girl who once made everyone laugh? This wasn't just because I wanted to fit in; it was so much more than that. It was more like culture shock, and I wasn't prepared for it. I thought I could seamlessly be the same me as I was in high school. Yet in retrospect, it sounds ridiculous. How could I be the same me when everything was different? Even through this angst, I was growing. I was getting out there and challenging myself. It was simply ridiculous to cling to the past. I wasn't that version of "me" anymore.

When I finally looked past the self-sabotage and realized what I was doing, I felt so embarrassed by my behavior. I thought I was so much stronger than that. Yet, I was completely worn out. My spirit was silenced (as corny as that sounds). So what did I do? What could I do? I pulled back. I asked myself what I needed to do to get back to smiling, back to laughing, back to just breathing easy. I figured out this was much larger than what I could handle and looked to every resource I could find. I found out that I was struggling with my self-confidence and needed an extreme boost to my self-esteem. The more information I read, the more I found out that so many girls go through the same thing—and they were just like me. Suddenly, I didn't feel alone.

A SELF-CONFIDENCE OVERHAUL

First step, get outside your head. Reach out to your campus health center and see if they offer some form of mental health service. If they don't, ask if there are organizations on campus that do. Therapy is one of life's greatest untapped resources. It's great to have an outside element that you can spill your guts to. Plus, let's face it: you may not be hiding the world's greatest secret, but you still may not want your friends to know exactly what's going on. Heck, *you* may not even know what's really going on! Working with a therapist will allow for your anxieties to become tangible so they can be worked on, instead of just a mess of emotions trapped inside your head.

Your therapist could suggest ways to work with your issues and provide strategies to overcome difficult situations. They also help you focus on what's really troubling you, and will troubleshoot based on particular problems instead of giving a general diagnosis that would otherwise just mute the problem instead of making it go away. If you're unsure if you "need" therapy, chances are you do. Therapy isn't for the "crazy," the weak, or the otherwise helpless. It's for the everyday girl who may be punishing herself for things she can't control. A friend of mine explained, "I feel as if my problems aren't big enough" to seek outside help. But they are! There are no silly questions, and I think the important thing to recognize is that they are there to help you. They provide an extra hand when you feel as if you're juggling a basketload of issues.

Many experts say to try out one session. And keep in mind that choosing a therapist is like choosing a great pair of sunglasses—not all will fit. Sometimes you have to try several pairs but when it works, it works. Some therapists just don't click with your personality and that's OK. Some people like their therapist to be very strict and straight-laced; others like to feel as if they're talking to a friend. Try out a session with someone you like, and if you still leave uneasy, at least you can say you tried.

What worked for me was a kind of conditioning that is both a mix of Kimora Lee Simmons's fabulousness and a tad of weepy Dr. Phil. There needs to be some concrete work to build up your mind and your self-esteem, but there also needs to be something to speak to your spirit. Remind yourself that you are fabulous and carry your own set of idiosyncrasies that make you who you are.

Embrace them! These are the things people love about you. When you're feeling down, try to find something positive to affirm about yourself. Finding something positive will remind you that there are things that you love about yourself, which will combat the hate-speak you may say on a daily basis.

Believe it or not, the more times you say that you're a screwup, the more likely you will end up believing it. At the very least, ask yourself, "Would you talk to a friend the same way you talk to yourself?" Chances are if you did, you wouldn't have any friends. People who suffer from low self-esteem issues judge themselves to such a higher degree that they don't realize that they are their own worst enemy.

TYPICAL ROADBLOCKS

Once you have seemed to hammer out a system that works for you, it's time to apply it and see how it holds up in the real world. A lot of work goes into recognizing the damage we put on ourselves, and then figuring out the best way to repair the damage. However, the work doesn't stop once you've worked out the equation—now it's time to apply the system and test its effectiveness.

While we discussed major self-confidence overhaul, most of the time it's the little things that can have even the most confident chicas checking their self-esteem at the door. There are moments when you just sort of hit an emotional snag, and need some extra support to get you through it.

Post-breakup

We've all been there. The sniffling, the Facebook stalking, the masochistic viewing of *The Notebook*. Breaking up sucks and it often gives your self-esteem a beating. After a breakup, the most common things women look for are answers. We try to categorize blame, we scrutinize our faults, harp on our shortcomings, and it really does a number on us. During this time, try to celebrate your newfound single status. Make a list of all the qualities you love about yourself. Sure, it's easy to list all the bad qualities of your ex, but it isn't about him, it's about you. Take the time to get to know yourself better, and enjoy the spontaneity of being single.

BFF no more (breakup with a girlfriend)

Breaking up sucks, but what happens when you break up with a friend? I'd rather sit through a million sappy romantic comedies with a best friend than watch my favorite movie alone. Breaking it off with a BFF can be really rough, especially since we rely on them when things aren't going right. During these years, relationships will be tested, and if comes to a point when you and your true blue aren't working out, you may drift apart. Just like any relationship, take the time to mourn the loss of your bond and get it out of your system, but also start reaching out to the other friends in your circle. Then try to reach out to people you may not have talked to before. Ask the girl down the hall about the song she plays that you totally love, or hang out with your lab partner after class. Get involved in your student government or your campus paper. While it sucks to lose the Paris to your Nicole, it doesn't mean you've lost all the cool things that make you who you are.

Change in physical appearance (weight loss, weight gain, zits, etc.)

College is a time where you'll be testing your mind and your body, and you may notice your body changing as you spend more time away from home. If you see yourself losing or gaining an alarming amount of weight, try to reflect on your routine and your eating habits, as stressful eating may pinpoint an underlying issue. If you're concerned, talk to a nutritionist or a doctor about a healthy diet, but remember nobody's perfect, and no one is expecting you to be either.

Failed an exam/class

Remember that all-nighter? The one last week, where you had to miss your best friend's band and the midnight waffle sale to spend the entire night cramming for that bio exam? The one you were studying for for about a week? Yeah, it just came back, and you totally bombed. So, not only did you miss the killer encore but it was all for nothing. Yikes! Nothing is worse than putting your all into an assignment and finding out you failed. The first thing you should do is find out why you bombed so you can put it to rest. Look over your paper or your exam and really review your work—learn what mistakes you made so you don't make them again. If you feel shortchanged, schedule a time to talk with your professor to discuss your performance. The most important thing here is to make the progress tangible. In most cases a make-up test isn't an option, but the work you put into understanding your mistakes will help you with other assignments down the line. Reviewing your test or paper and learning from it helps channel your stress into something productive, which is way better than just throwing in the towel.

FINDING AN EQUILIBRIUM

When I finally pieced myself back together, I was able to see the person I was truly becoming. It's easy to get over a cold, but not so easy to recover from being emotionally under the weather. You can't just snap back to "normal"—and really, why would you want to? You've been through the hard part so try to think of ways of how it can work for you. We mess up, we goof off, and it's all just part of the game. Half the fun in making mistakes is the laughs that are brought on along the way.

staying fit in college

Donyel L. Griffin, Kean University

veryone fears those evil, infamous "freshman fifteen," but are they really fact or just fiction? Leading a healthy lifestyle can be hard in college when you are always on the run and Mom isn't there with all three of your daily meals prepared. Classes, jobs, extracurricular activities, and your social life can cause your eating habits to go haywire.

Last semester when I was an intern, I'd come back from my internship and feel the urge to devour something easy and quick. I'd rarely eat lunch during the day, as I was busy on my feet, working on projects and helping editors into the early evening. When I arrived back on campus I was tired and hungry. My solution? I would grab the easiest food like a greasy Hot Pocket or fries for dinner. Sometimes I'd try to be healthy with a sandwich or salad or something sensible. But most of the time I used my crazy workload as an excuse to eat certain "bad" foods a little too much. As an incoming college student, you too will be busy. However, if you take control early on, you can develop great habits that can last a lifetime. If you want to win the "Freshman Fitness Test," here are a few tips to help you stay fit by eating better meals and staying healthier overall.

YOUR FIRST YEAR

As a new college student, it's only normal that you will have a million questions. Simple things like where to get food, where can you work out, how much to spend, and how to stay on top of things can seem overwhelming when you first arrive at your new home. So let's get started.

Eating right

Most likely, you will have a university cafeteria, and the majority of you who live on campus will have meal plans. As a freshman at my school, I was required to have a meal plan of $1,200 per semester because freshmen dorms did not have kitchens. Meal plans are usually required for freshmen and have been included in your tuition bill. These days, college students access their meal plans through their University Identification Card, which swipes almost like a credit card in cafeterias and dining halls. Some universities have dining halls that are like cafeterias but are buffet-style and have an all-you-can-eat theme. Proceed with caution with buffets! Sometimes too many food options are not a good thing; overabundance can lead to overeating. But rest assured that you can eat healthy with minimal effort. These places almost always have vegetarian dishes, salads, and fruits for health-conscious students. Some colleges have meal cards where you can go off campus to local restaurants and they will deduct money from your meal card while others have student discounts at nearby restaurants. Here's a healthy tip: instead of going crazy at the nearby McDonald's, or KFC, look for other options like Salad Works, Subway, or alternative restaurants like sushi bars and Thai food, which offer healthier meal choices and place less of an emphasis on fried, fattening foods. But watch out for that shrimp tempura at the sushi restaurant! Check to see if the restaurant has nutritional guidelines where you can find out just exactly how many calories are in that delectable item you're getting ready to order.

Working out

During your first week, find your school's gym. Recreation hall or gym facility fees are usually included in your tuition bill, so you might as well use it! I cannot tell you how excited I was my junior year when my university finally completed our new gym. It was closer to the dorms than the previous gym, and the new state-of-the-art treadmills with TVs were definitely an upgrade!

Did you know that you can even get school credit for working out? At most schools, you can. Have you always been curious about Tae Kwon Do or would like to become a better swimmer? Check out your school's course offerings and sign up for an easy A and better body next semester.

What if you don't live on campus? Sorry, no excuse. You still have access to the gym before and after class or on the weekends. Even though you may not have the opportunity to work out several times a week, a regular routine of two or three times per week will help you see results. One year, my roommate and I did weekly Tae Bo workouts in our dorm room. Sure, we were lucky to have a spacious area that year. But no matter how big or small your dorm room is, make use of what you've got, whether it's your school's running track, the gym, or your own dorm room. Bottom line: find a routine that works with you and your schedule and stick with it!

DON'T FREAK OUT

So you've been at school for a few months, and really haven't gotten into a healthy routine yet. If you look in the mirror and don't like what you see, stop the negative feelings! Don't freak out if you're not at the same weight you were when you first started high school. What many women fail to realize is when you first enter college at 17 or 18, your body is still developing physically. So you can't compare your body to how it was a few years ago or sometimes even a few months ago!

Take a deep breath, and refocus your efforts on starting a healthy routine of exercising and eating right. Also, being healthy isn't just about the numbers on your scale; there are several other tests that are used to determine how fit you really are. Body mass index, or BMI, is a guideline used to judge whether you are at risk for health problems associated with your weight. Rather than relying on the bathroom scale, experts say that you should also know your BMI, a figure that takes into account not just weight but height to indicate body fat. In general, experts say that you should aim for a BMI that's over 18 and under 25. (To check your BMI try the online calculator at www.healthcentral.com/diet-exercise/index-1688-143.html) You may be surprised to find that you are *under*weight when you consider your height and body frame.

STOP BEING LAZY

OK, so you've made the decision to get healthy. Now the question is how to do it.

Staying healthy is more about choosing not to be lazy than anything else. Lazy is having the time and means to go work out but choosing not to because you'd rather watch *America's Next Top Model*. If that's the case, pick a different time to work out or record your favorite show. I know from experience that sometimes my friends and I would use a TV show or some other reason as an excuse not to go to the gym. Once a friend of mine even said, "I don't want to walk to the gym because it's raining outside! Guess I can't work out today." I'm not saying become a gym fanatic or anything, but if you have the time, why not go? The hardest part of working out is getting yourself to the gym. I promise that you'll feel fantastic afterward.

Some of you may end up living off campus or in apartment-style dorms. If you have a kitchen with a stove, jump for joy! Your options are endless. All you need to do is visit your supermarket right away and start cooking your own meals. Cooking your own meals has two benefits: it's generally healthier *and* it's cheaper. Sometimes it will be tempting to go to Applebee's or the local diner for a quick bite, but don't cave in to a quick and unhealthy fix. And don't forget that ordering Chinese food and pizza can become really pricey on a student's limited budget.

Make cooking at home fun! Invite your friends to your place for a low-cost and healthy dinner. One of my former roommates and I used to occasionally cook dinner together and make a recipe of baked chicken with breadcrumbs and usually a vegetable like green beans or broccoli to go with it. It was filling, full of flavor, and more health-friendly than eating pizza and french fries. For other recipes, a great book to pick up is *The Complete Idiot's Guide to the College Diet Cookbook* by Shelly Vaughan James, which also includes recipes tested by students at four major universities.

FIND A SYSTEM THAT WORKS FOR YOU

The best way to get healthy is to establish a routine and stick with it. Take your daily planner or even a blank piece of paper and write down your schedule. Include class, work, and any other obligations you have. Next, find spots where you could fit in a workout; it doesn't have to be every day. You'll probably have some Monday/Wednesday/Friday classes with breaks in between. Just pencil in an hour at the gym at the same time for each of these days, and treat it like a class. When you set a routine, you'll be more likely to stick to your workout plan. Also, don't worry if you go off track. Maybe that's an indication that you need to rethink your schedule, and you shouldn't be afraid to readjust.

Since I hate the word "diet" (and you'll find out why later on), think about a program that doesn't tell you what to eat, but encourages you to make better decisions. My friend currently is on the Weight Watchers plan and says it works for her because she can eat all the foods she likes but just in moderation.

Working out with friends is a great way to stay motivated. You will be much more likely to go to the gym when someone is depending on you to be there. But just make sure you first discuss your goals and what type of workouts you are going to do. For example, I had a friend who inherited her workout routine from her boyfriend who was involved in track. Needless to say, her complete routine was difficult! It consisted of a long warm up, and then a lot of running on the track. Now, I had no qualms about warm-ups and doing exercises, but I have always despised running. This is an important thing to remember. Having friends to help you exercise or eat healthier can be a huge motivator, but you have to make sure not to lose track of your *own* goals. A friend may want to lose a few pounds while you'd like to lose 20. That's a *big* difference. Or maybe your roommate can eat whatever she wants and still maintain her hourglass figure with just exercise while you have to exercise *and* eat better to stay in shape. Everyone's body type is different, so before you try to mirror your friends' habits, find the system that works the best for you!

> ### Dating Someone?
>
> Some of you can become unhealthy by association. One of my close friends started dating her boyfriend over a year ago, and since then, she's noticed she gained a few pounds from eating out more often. The problem? She feels the need to clean her plate just as he does, and most restaurants are notorious for their extra-large servings. It's not a myth that men can eat more than women and still maintain a reasonable weight.
>
> It's cool to dine out with your boyfriend or even a bunch of your guy friends, but realize that while he can scarf down 8 slices of pizza and seem not to gain a pound, it's definitely not a habit to acquire. However, don't be too afraid or shy to eat around your guy. Most likely, he'd rather see you actually enjoy food and eat well than pretend you hate food. In fact, your good habits might inspire him to make a few positive changes for himself!

BE REALISTIC

Finally, the trick to being healthy and fit in college is getting rid of the word "diet" and substituting the words "moderation" and "exercise." I know that the latest diet crazes are everywhere—in gossip magazines, the news, and commercials. I don't care how often you read about it because dieting is not a healthy way to eat long-term. You may lose a few pounds initially, but they always come back unless you change your lifestyle. UCLA researchers recently found that one year after starting a diet, people were no better off than before—in fact, about half of them ended up gaining weight. Get rid of the word "diet" because restricting your eating is not healthy in the long term!

Make realistic changes to your lifestyle that can be made over time and do everything in moderation. Only you know what you can handle. For instance, if you entirely abandon a food that you love because it's unhealthy, your supposedly healthy change may not last long. It's very difficult to give up favorite foods. It might make you more likely to binge or go overboard later.

I'll give you a quick example of what I mean by moderation. You're going to make a sandwich. Instead of a glob of mayo to top it off, use something healthier like mustard or even fat-free mayo. Or try eating only half the sandwich. And when it comes to snacking, instead of having a candy bar every day after class, cut down to giving yourself this treat once a week while filling yourself up with tasty fruits and vegetables on the other days. If you find yourself having to eat out every week, cut it down to maybe once or twice a month.

Be safe

Being healthy is great, but don't go to the extreme and acquire an eating disorder. Eating disorders such as bulimia, anorexia, binge eating, and overeating can happen to anyone. Actually, 5–7% of women in the United States will suffer from some type of eating disorder during their lifetime. Also, something else to watch out for is overexercising. Some warning signs of a compulsive exerciser are the following: exercising even when you don't feel well, basing your daily diet on how much you exercise, constantly worrying you'll gain weight if you don't exercise every day, forcing yourself to do multiple workouts during the day, or becoming depressed if you miss a workout. If you think you've acquired any of these unhealthy eating or lifestyle habits, seek out professional help. This is something you do not want to ignore, because it may become worse over time, negatively affecting your collegiate experience and your health.

LAST BIT OF ADVICE

Remember that you're in college, so expect late-night pizza orders or times when you'll pig out on ice cream and cookies. Food is not to be feared. Your best bet to ensuring a successful college experience is to enjoy your favs in moderation and exercise throughout the week. With this approach, you will be the best you can be academically, socially, and physically.

the dangers of eating disorders

*Aja Johnson, University of Maryland–
College Park*

Eating is an important part of your health while in college. Unlike being at home in high school when there is a strict time for breakfast, lunch, and dinner, in college you can pig out at lunch and then have brownies for dinner. Nothing about college life is regulated in a way to mark which behaviors are normal, odd, or bordering on disordered. That is why it is so difficult to know when it's time to seek help for what may be an eating disorder.

The concept of eating disorders may not be entirely new, as you might have learned about them through a high school health class or even during a "very special" episode of your favorite teen sitcom. While we might know what eating disorders are, it's important to understand how they function on a college campus and what to do if you or someone you know suffers from disordered eating.

WHAT IS DISORDERED EATING?

In such a weight-conscious society, it's hard to distinguish what's harmless and what's dangerous. Eating disorders are extreme eating patterns that have a psychological dependency on control.

There are three main types: anorexia nervosa, bulimia nervosa, and binge-eating disorder. Anorexia nervosa is the excessive starving or limiting of food. This can be aided with the use of medication or extreme dieting, with girls losing weight at rapid speed. Bulimia nervosa follows a routine of bingeing and purging. Bingeing consists of eating a large amount of food in one sitting, followed by purging, which is ridding the body of this food in an extreme manner (via vomiting or through the use of laxatives). Binge-eating is simply using food as a means of comfort, consuming large amounts of food rapidly in one sitting. Unlike bulimia, there is no purging process.

It may be hard to spot someone who is suffering from disordered eating, as they don't always look extremely skinny. Sufferers of bulimia especially may look overweight, and may view bulimia as a "weight maintenance" practice. Girls can develop a combination of these disorders, jumping from one to another at any given time.

THE LESSER-KNOWN DISORDERS ON CAMPUS

While these disorders are often seen on college campuses, there are also new forms of these behaviors that are attacking young women. Exercise-bulimia, where exercising takes the place of traditional purging, is silently afflicting college students and no one really knows how to treat it. Since exercising is seen as a healthy activity, one wouldn't assume that it could act as a disease. However, this follows the same pattern of overdoing it, where the length of exercise becomes excessive, with a woman (or man!) working out for hours and hours on end. In this case, exercising works just as any other traditional form of purging, with the intent to work away any food the individual consumed.

There are also more dangerous forms of disordered eating that feed off of the use of drugs or binge drinking. In this type, controlled substances are used as a way to numb the body for its need for food, blurring the individual's perception of self. While exercise-bulimia revamps the way we look at bulimia, drugs and alcohol respond to the depressive state the individual is in. The drug and alcohol use compounds the effects of the lack of eating, and can destroy the body at a much quicker speed. In these cases, it's important to refer to the motive of action. Disordered eating is not just about starving yourself, or vomiting, but about the reasons behind these actions. Experiencing extreme feelings of guilt, sadness, anger, or remorse follows these actions, and can signal disordered eating.

These retooled versions of traditional eating disorders become almost more dangerous than the former, as they take away the focus of the behavior. While it's easy to spot individuals following unorthodox patterns of behavior, it becomes difficult when the behavior appears "normal." This makes it harder for the abuser to identify exactly what the behavior is doing. Overexercising and facilitating disordered eating habits with controlled substances are problems, but when paired with low self-esteem, and a crippling body image, these actions become part of a much larger problem. Eating disorders arise from depression, anxiety, and overwhelming feelings of being out of control. The food is representative of something larger than just raw material. Although there are issues of self-esteem, weight-management, and self-worth, the disorder thrives off of the satisfaction of completing a goal, attaining a certain ideal, adhering to a larger standard of beauty.

WORRIED ABOUT A FRIEND?

If you suspect that a friend suffers from disordered eating, keep on the lookout for her behavior. Watch for girls who suddenly become withdrawn, secretive, or moody. If you hear a friend making negative remarks about her body and/or image, idolizing or glorifying thinness, and you notice a shift in her behavior, then she may be suffering from a disorder. If a friend has a history of depression, physical/sexual abuse, or weight issues, she may be more at risk to rebound or partake in disordered eating. While it may be awkward to approach a friend about her eating habits, it's important to confront disordered behavior before it spirals out of control.

Set yourself up in a place that may be comforting to her, and be direct with your concerns. A simple "I've noticed you've been feeling down lately, and I haven't seen you eat much and I'm concerned." This addresses the behavior, but does it in a way where she doesn't feel attacked. Avoid blame or guilt, and just stick to your own observations and feelings. Present options to her to put her in control of the situation. If the direct approach is too difficult, frame it in the sense of a hypothetical issue. Ask for her reaction to a show on eating disorders or a special documentary. Expressing your support for this "hypothetical" situation may clue her in that you're a safe source for her to talk to. Be sure to follow up, and let her know that you're there to help in any way you can. What you want to do is offer a safe place and support.

Your own behavior

If you feel that your eating habits are sliding toward the unhealthy, try to assess what your behavior means. Recognizing disordered eating is the first step on the road to recovery. There are plenty of resources out there in order to understand your disease. Talk to a therapist about your behavior. They can work out a plan for you to understand and work with your disease. The best thing you can do is focus on your health and rebuild what the disorder damaged (self-confidence and self-esteem).

If you're unsure if you're experiencing disordered eating, listen to your body. Give yourself extra attention during periods of stress or depression. It's easy to feel trapped by fad diets and quick pills, but the results of these behaviors are long lasting and can have terrible effects on your body. If you're truly unsatisfied with your appearance, talk with your doctor and discuss healthy alternatives to weight loss and management. There are plenty of healthy ways to get big results. Be sure to tune in to the reasons why you want to lose weight. Weight loss other than for the sake of your health sets unrealistic expectations and can lead to dangerous behavior patterns. Consult a therapist to understand what such a change can do to your mental health.

If you are concerned about yourself or a friend, contact the National Eating Disorder Association's Helpline, at 800-931-2237.

U Chic Essentials—Healthy and Happy

Listen to your body

College is the time to do anything and everything. But be careful not to overexert yourself. Take time to rest and rejuvenate. It will remind you that you are important, hardworking, and deserve to be pampered every now and then.

Remember that you are beautiful!

Cherish your unique beauty both inside and out. Ignore the tabloids that say all of Hollywood is getting plastic surgery these days. They are chasing an unreal beauty expectation that does not end up being beautiful but, well, boring.

Use your on-campus resources

From the campus health center to the fitness center, your university has fantastic resources created specifically for you. And you're paying for them, so why not use them? Your body and mind will thank you.

Looking for more great advice? Head to www.UniversityChic.com and look for "U Chic Picks!" for our fav resources and websites—they come highly recommended from our guide's contributors and editors. Be sure to leave your suggestions as well!

CHAPTER 9

Surviving Temptation Island

ollege is the ultimate Temptation Island. No curfews. No limits on alcohol or Facebook. No reminders to do homework. We could go on, but you get the picture. The only hard and steadfast rule is that you are in charge, and no one is there to help you say "no" to the many temptations that you'll face. Sometimes, it's not your own temptations that should be of concern. Your friends, a boyfriend, a guy that you just met at a bar, and maybe even a professor will face their own temptations, and might drag you into situations you never had planned (or wanted) to be in. Taken too far, something that started out as innocent could end up being a disaster for all. Follow the advice in this chapter, and you'll learn how to not only survive but also thrive on Temptation Island.

over-the-top party pals and ways to deal

Erica Strauss, Kent State University

erfectly straightened hair? Check. Super-cute new outfit, complete with matching shoes and bag? Check. Your best friend completely plastered before you even head out the door? Uh-oh. Partying with the girls is a great way to de-stress after a tiring week of classes, papers, and exams. And if you haven't heard it before, "College is the time to try everything," and "Hey, you only live once!" While college is known as a time for experimenting, there is still work to be done and, well, embarrassing moments to be had.

Whether hitting a hot bar or club or hanging at a frat party, these moments, although fun, can also pose some challenges if you've got a friend who parties a little too hard. So maybe you're not the drunk girl dancing on the stripper pole, puking in the bathroom sink, or making out with a random stranger—*but what do you do if one of your friends is?*

Whether you're finally checking out the frat house down the street known for throwing killer bashes, kicking it with a few friends on the front porch, or hitting up the bar scene, keep these tips in mind when you're hanging out with a friend who tends to drink a little too much and take things a little too far.

SO, SHE'S EMBARRASSING YOU
You're at a bar

Is she letting a little too loose on the stripper pole? She might not be the sexiest chick on the dance floor after her seventh beer, but now probably isn't the time to discuss her not-so-suave moves. As long as she isn't popping, locking, and dropping in a way you know would embarrass her if she was sober, let it go. Everyone deserves the chance to go a little crazy on occasion. However, there's a fine line between being a fun drunk and a drunken mess. Use your best judgment in determining that line. If your gut tells you she's gone a little too far (i.e., taking clothes off), don't hesitate to let her know.

You're at a house/frat party with strangers

Is she making out with a dark shadowy figure off in a deserted corner? In college, a few random make-out sessions are almost a rite of passage. But if things look seriously wrong (for example, that guy she's kissing in the corner is twice her age, she's promising to go home with a boy from her English class, or announcing that she's driving home completely smashed), it's time for a chat. In these situations, it's OK to step in to help your friend avoid some potentially horrible consequences. They may drunkenly claim they hate you at the time, but they'll love you for it tomorrow.

DON'T, UNDER ANY CIRCUMSTANCES, LET HER LEAVE BY HERSELF!

Here are a couple of scenarios that you may face when partying with your over-the-top party pal. This is by no means an exhaustive list. For more input on what to do in other scenarios, visit the discussion boards at www.universitychic.com/guidediscussion.

If it's just the two of you

So that boy from her class? He says there's something going on at his house later and invites your friend, and you, along. You're tired and so ready for bed—but your friend obviously isn't. Make sure you let her know that you aren't going to follow her and that you don't think she's capable of going by herself. It may seem a little aggressive. But even if you weren't invited, it's still your responsibility to make sure she gets home safely. Offer an alternative: how about a few of you go out for some late-night pizza? The extra calories aren't half as dangerous as heading back to an almost-stranger's house.

If you're out with a group

Partying with a group changes the dynamic slightly. You should weigh all the options. Do you or any of your friends know this guy? Do you have any mutual friends? Does one of the other girls want to go with your friend, and is she sober enough to make rational decisions? Don't be afraid to play Mom in the group. Remember that nagging little voice you hear inside your head when you're about to do something you know is wrong? Be the one to speak the truth: going home with this guy is reckless, and could be dangerous.

If you just met up with her

Say you didn't spend three hours primping with her and didn't even know she was going to be at the same place, but you happen to bump into her at the party. Although there may not be an obligation, a good friend should keep an eye on her intoxicated girlfriend. Offer her the same options mentioned above and advise her as you would any of the girls you came with. If she does decide to leave with a guy she just met in her drunken state, check up on her later. For instance, give her cell phone a ring and make sure she doesn't need an easy out or somewhere else to stay.

If she's attempting to drive

The statistics are haunting—1,700 college students between the ages of 18 and 24 die each year from alcohol-related unintentional injuries. This includes vehicle crashes. Don't let your friend become a statistic! Offer to pay for a cab to send her home. Walk home with her and promise a ride back to her car the next morning. Do whatever it takes to make sure she doesn't get her keys in the ignition.

STAY CALM

You've decided to help, but what happens when your friend is not eagerly responding to your advice? Remember that your friend is in an altered state of mind. This means that anything you say or do at this point could be blown out of proportion. She might not take your advice so lightly, especially if she's intoxicated. Don't get angry with her or give up. Although she may not realize it, she probably needs your help. Explain that you are only letting her know because you are trying to be a good friend. Leave it at that. There's no reason to fight with her when she probably won't even remember why she was mad in the morning. Plus, no one wants to cause a scene when they're out having a good time.

NOW SHE'S PUKING ALL OVER THE FLOOR!

You've managed to talk your friend into doing the right thing in choosing to leave the bar and go home. But your job doesn't end there. If your friend is extremely wasted, don't leave your plastered pal passed out on the tile. Get her some water and hold her hair back. Then get her in bed on her stomach. Don't forget that she could possibly choke if she is lying on her back. She'll thank you in the morning, even if she's uber-hungover.

YOUR FRIEND IS COMPLETELY WASTED AND NOW YOU'RE REALLY WORRIED

If her breathing slows, she appears unconscious, or her skin is cold and clammy, she might have alcohol poisoning. Don't hesitate to dial 911 or find a Resident Assistant who will do it for you. At Princeton, university policy requires that students help severely drunk people by contacting local medical or safety personnel or local police. And don't worry. Neither you nor the people you help will be disciplined for intoxication. Even if your school does not have this policy, always take care of a friend in need.

A COMMON OCCURRENCE?

People can develop psychological and physical dependency on alcohol, and alcoholism can occur in people as early as college. It's not uncommon at all. In fact, 31% of college students meet criteria for substance abuse and 6% meet the criteria for alcohol dependence. Everybody likes to have fun and relax in his or her own way after a long, stressful week. But if your friend is drinking every night, drinking alone, or can't control or stop herself while she is drinking, she could be developing alcoholism. You'll be doing her a favor if you sit down and talk to her about her drinking.

NEED MORE INFORMATION ON ALCOHOLISM?

Check out www.alcoholism.about.com for tons of information about alcoholism and other forms of substance abuse, including an Alcohol Abuse screening quiz.

staying safe on campus

Monica Taylor, California State University – Los Angeles

A few months after I moved into the dorms, a young woman was sexually assaulted in my housing complex. My friend Hailey and I were concerned that the word was not getting out to the rest of the campus, and decided to try to do something about it on our own. We spent a whole day running around campus, and were sent from office to office trying to talk to the right person that would help us get the word out. Luckily, we were able to convince campus police to make us hundreds of copies of the crime report. Hailey and I proceeded to post them in every housing building, on every door. This was an unfortunate crash course introduction on the importance of being safe on campus.

WHY SAFETY MATTERS

College students, especially female college students, need to learn how to be safe on their campus. Why? We can simply flip open the *LA Times* to find an article about a woman being shot outside a party in East LA. Or the story of a woman being shot and then pushed out a window. From the headlines to music videos, physical violence—especially against women—is just a part of everyday life in our culture. The result of this is that the college campus is not always a safe place for female students. In face of this, we need to take control of our lives and our safety, and learn how to be as safe as possible. Now this does not mean that women have to walk around scared or survive in a state of fear. I believe women are capable of living their lives fully and being safe at the same time.

DO WE BRING IT ON?

Before I dive into the practical areas of campus safety, let me say that although there are ways to ensure one's safety on campus, any type of violence against women is *never*, in any circumstance, their fault. Women don't deserve assault or anything else because they left a window open or walked home late at night or wore an extra tiny skirt. Violence against a woman is never her fault. With that noted, here's how you can make your college experience safer.

UTILIZE YOUR CAMPUS RESOURCES

An important first step in keeping yourself safe on campus is recognizing the value of resources available on your campus. Most campuses have escort services—use them. If you get out of class late in the evening or stay a little later to talk with your professor, you can call a number and have someone to walk you wherever you're going. Don't be concerned that you might be wasting anyone's time to walk you even a few blocks to your car. The campus security officer's job is to be there for you at all times.

> One time, I was on campus after eleven working on a project. I didn't even bother considering how I could walk home safely alone. Instead, I called campus police for an escort, and they actually sent an officer in a police car to drive me down to my dorm. Program the number into your cell phone for the escort services on campus, so you are never stuck walking alone at night.

There are several other things to be aware of when considering your safety on campus. Be aware of the lighting on your campus. Are all areas of the campus and your dorms well-lit? Are there large dark areas? You want to be in lighted areas at all times of the night. And if there are major areas lacking sufficient lighting, make a stink about it. It will take persistence to get these things fixed, but you deserve safety. Your campus should additionally provide emergency phones. They should be sporadically placed around the campus for you to grab and call in case of any emergency. Know where they are. Finally, be aware of any large bushes. Are there large bushes and shrubbery that would make the perfect hiding place for someone? Knowing where these bushes are and the potentially dangerous situations they may present is important to keeping yourself safe.

DORM ROOM SAFETY

Now, regarding the dorms, keep windows and doors locked. End of story. This is probably tricky to do, as people are always going in and out of other people's rooms and whatnot, but it's essential to keeping yourself safe. And don't be afraid to ask your roommate(s) to do the same. Roomies should look out for one another. My last bit of advice on keeping yourself safe on campus: have your campus police number programmed into your cell and if you have a landline, on the speed dial. My speed dial number seven says "Campus Popo." This way the police are always at your fingertips in case of emergency.

TAKE A SELF-DEFENSE COURSE

If you have not already done so, sign up for a self-defense class as soon as you arrive on campus. Now, I'm not claiming that if you take one of these classes that you will have the ability to beat the crap out of every person who steps in your path. However, it does equip you with the tools to defend yourself, to fight back, to get away from an assailant. Also, it isn't just about the physical aspect of defense—like how to use a man's strength against him so you can get away—but there is also a psychological component. After taking the course, I feel stronger and more confident in my ability to defend myself. It's not just how to drop and elbow some guy in the cajones when he bear hugs you from the back. It's empowerment. My campus offered Rape Aggression Defense classes in the dorms, and also a Women's Self-Defense class through the kinesiology department. Look into your resources on campus. See what's offered and take advantage.

By preparing and knowing what it takes to be safe, you are increasing the chances that you will not have to experience one of those shocking stories. You deserve to feel safe on your campus. Be aware, know what resources are available, and take those self-defense classes—every last one of them! Safety is a major issue on college campuses that women have to deal with in a way that men don't. So educate yourself, and be empowered. We college women are completely capable of being safe, fun, young, adventurous, and wise all at the same time.

dangerous dependency:
prescription drugs

Erica Strauss, Kent State University

etween five-page papers, exhausting lecture halls, endless pages of math problems, and weekend road trips, the life of a college student can be overwhelming. There are lots of ways to reduce stress: exercise, yoga, meditation, writing, to name just a few. But some college students turn to prescription drugs instead. Bad idea. For one, they're illegal unless you're the one with the prescription. And two, they're incredibly addictive.

Need to get that paper done in an hour? Pop an Adderall. Want to unwind after a nerve-racking presentation? Try a Xanax. Have a few aches and pains? Vicodin will do the trick. OK, not really...

"Marie" (not her real name), a junior fine arts major, takes Adderall, a popular prescription drug, for her ADHD symptoms. Adderall is a stimulant that affects chemicals in the brain and controls hyperactivity. "I take it because I can't concentrate without it," she said. However, many college students take drugs that aren't prescribed to them as a way to easily ace exams, chill out at a big frat party, or even clean their dorm rooms.

Over the years, students have started to use drugs in ways doctors never could have imagined. Adderall has been described as the drug for overachievers, and the side effects—including increased energy, ability to focus, and inability to sleep—sound like a miracle pill for the busy, hectic, fast-paced life of a college student.

"Whenever I have a paper due, I won't stress about it because I know I can take Adderall and get it done fast," said a freshman who wishes to remain anonymous. "It also helps when I pull all-nighters to study for exams." Adderall also suppresses the user's appetite, and many students, especially young women, enjoy that extra side effect.

"I like it because it's like taking Stackers or other diet pills, but you can also concentrate," she said. Not only will you get an A on your exam, but—hey!—you could even drop a dress size.

But Adderall is not the only drug abused on campuses. Xanax, Valium, and Vicodin—which treat anxiety, pain, and insomnia, among other ailments—are also college favorites. And with rising cases of generalized anxiety disorder on college campuses, according to the Anxiety Disorders Association of America, many students are finding themselves with easy access to these pills. Just ask the kid sitting behind you in psych, your hall-mate, or even that gorgeous girl in your sorority—one of them probably has a prescription to your drug of choice, or knows someone who does.

"People know I have a prescription, and I get phone calls all the time from people asking for it," Marie said. "I don't need them all, so usually I'll just give them away."

Marie isn't the only legally prescribed drug user who chooses to sell or give away her pills. A study conducted earlier this year by a Massachusetts psychopharmacologist reported that 11% of students surveyed who had prescriptions to Adderall XR sold their pills. Another 22% reported misusing their prescription and didn't take the pills when they were supposed to.

THE DANGERS

Although Marie is prescribed the drug, she can still see the many dangers of drug misuse. She feels not only physically, but also psychologically, dependent on the drug.

The drug becomes a crutch—an easy way to avoid a bigger issue. Didn't attend enough lectures? Take an Adderall and you can read the chapter in two hours. Want to calm your nerves before you get your drink on at the bars? Take a Valium to get an extra buzz. The problem is that once the drugs wear off, the real issues are still there.

"I feel like I can't do my work without Adderall now," Marie said. "I think people who take drugs recreationally take the pills to escape their problems. They're just looking for a quick fix for whatever is wrong at the time."

Many students don't see the harm in popping a pill that is prescribed to someone else. People mistakenly believe that it's OK to take the drugs because they have been prescribed by a doctor, according to a study published in the *New England Journal of Medicine* in 2006. But when they are not prescribed to you in particular, you never know what kind of reaction your body might have when you introduce a new medication. Not only are there health risks involved, but addiction is another very serious side effect.

"I've seen a lot of people, good friends actually, become addicted to drugs that weren't prescribed for them," Marie said. "I've seen it ruin their lives."

But, prescription drugs don't carry the negative stigma like street drugs such as cocaine and heroin. You don't cringe to hear that a friend is taking excessive amounts of Adderall or Vicodin the way you would if they were hooked on cocaine.

"I take it to do better in school," said the same anonymous freshman. "It's not like I'm buying it off the street."

But getting caught with Adderall is just like getting caught with marijuana, since police can charge you with drug possession. And if you're caught selling your stash? Same deal: you can be charged with drug trafficking.

One acquaintance has never tried any prescription drugs because of the potential consequences. "I've heard of a bunch of people who do that stuff," she said. "I don't get it. I feel like if my doctor isn't the one who gave it to me, I don't want to take it." Goody-two-shoes? No. She's just smart. If you do not have a medical condition, you should not touch these things.

Despite the abuse of prescription drugs, the disorders mentioned in this article are real and do require treatment. If you feel that you suffer from ADHD or Generalized Anxiety Disorder, make an appointment with your doctor.

facing sexual harassment on campus

Monica Taylor, California State University – Los Angeles

S exual harassment on campus? That so does not happen anymore. Well, at least not to me anyways!" Does this sound like something you think when anyone mentions sexual harassment? Well, before you decide to skip to the next chapter, consider this: a recent research study by the American Association of University Women found that 62% of college women had experienced some form of sexual harassment. Surprised?

WHAT IS SEXUAL HARASSMENT, EXACTLY?

Before we dive any deeper into this discussion, it is worth asking what sexual harassment is in the first place. Definitions of sexual harassment vary depending on the source. I'm going to provide a definition from my own alma mater, California State University–Los Angeles that provides a policy statement regarding students' rights on campus. This definition is pretty standard and comprehensive.

Sexual harassment includes but is not limited to:

1. Unwanted sexual advances, request for sexual favors, and other verbal or physical conduct of a sexual nature.

2. Any act which contributes to a workplace or learning environment that is hostile, intimidating, offensive, or adverse to persons because of the sexual nature of the conduct.

3. Conditioning an act, decision, evaluation, or recommendation on the submission to or tolerance of any act of a sexual nature.

So to make it clear, sexual harassment is any form of unwanted sexual advances—touching or otherwise—which can be anything from someone grabbing your butt to making a sexual joke. It can also be any sexual act that interferes with your college environment or routine. For example, it's that guy who constantly talks about inappropriate sexual stuff around you, so you leave your dorm a few minutes early every morning to avoid seeing him. And finally, it includes someone who holds authority in your life, conditioning your success or advancement on your participating in anything sexual. So, for example, you have a professor who puts his hand on your thigh in his office and insinuates that your A in the class is dependant on you responding to his sexual advances. In short, anything sexual and unwanted by you is sexual harassment.

Sexual harassment presents a unique problem for women these days, especially since our culture tends to downplay the fact that it still exists. The college campus is no exception. Sexual harassment is common on college campuses, and women experience it in a distinctive way. According to the same AAUW study previously mentioned, women are more likely to be harassed through physical contact such as being touched, grabbed, or pinched. They are also more likely to receive sexual comments, gestures, jokes, or looks.

Bottom line: sexual harassment is not something that happens to other women somewhere out there. It happens to us—to you and me. Hopefully reading this will get you more informed and help you recognize it and know what to do when it happens.

> A recent American Association of University Women research study found that 62% of college women had experienced some form of sexual harassment. Surprised?

DON'T BE AFRAID TO SPEAK UP

Not only will you possibly face a sexual harasser at some point during college, people are going to try to make you feel like sexual harassment isn't that serious. They are going to tell you to let it go, to just ignore it, to stop complaining. They are going to tell you that it's excusable for this reason or that, and they are going to tell you that it doesn't really matter. Well, I want to tell you that those are all lies, absolute untruths, falsehoods that perpetuate our society's belief that disrespecting women is excusable. We live in a culture that views women as sex objects and devalues women constantly. Some men think they have a right to women sexually as if they are a possession, and that sexual harassment is excusable. Well it's not. Period.

Regardless of circumstance, please know that no one has a right to touch you, speak to you, or manipulate you in any unwanted sexual way.

> We live in a culture that views women as sex objects and devalues women constantly in the media. Some men think they have a right to women sexually as if they are a possession, and that sexual harassment is excusable.
> Well it's not. Period.

Responding to sexual harassment

So what in the world do you do when you're being sexually harassed? Part of the answer depends on who the harassment is coming from. Often sexual harassment is student-to-student. If it's happening in your dorm, tell your Resident Assistant, or your Resident Director. If it's from a staff member like a professor at your college, then many campuses have a designated person who receives sexual harassment complaints. Explore your university website to find contact information for that person and reach out to them as soon as possible. The longer you let it go, the less likely you'll find the courage to speak up. The common thread here is that you say something. Otherwise, they will continue violating your right to a life without harassment and most likely the rights of other women just like you. Speaking up about sexual harassment can be particularly difficult when that person is a peer or someone you have to see regularly. Being scared of retribution is commonplace. In my opinion, the best way to deal with this is by finding support in community. Friends, family, even staff on campus can offer you great support and encouragement when it seems like it's just too hard to deal with sexual harassment. Some friends may discourage you but real ones will stick with you through it. Also, be confident in yourself.

Reporting sexual harassment is just plain hard. If the person you report is a peer then you will probably see them around campus but don't be intimidated. You don't have to address them or talk to them or argue with them or explain yourself if you're not comfortable. Seek support within your community. No one has a right to sexually harass you in any way, and you have every right to defend yourself against inappropriate sexual behavior. Assert yourself. Don't be scared. And now that you know what sexual harassment is and that it's serious, you know how to deal.

Even though sexual harassment seems like something that doesn't happen any more, it's still a reality for many women in the workplace and on college campuses. But now that you have the info, you'll know what to do.

U Chic Essentials—Surviving Temptation Island

Be fearless

What you do and say influences your friends more than you think. When you fearlessly take the lead in defining your values and setting limits on drugs, alcohol, and other temptations, you'll find that those around you tend to follow. In the end, it helps everyone stay on track and out of trouble.

Sexual harassment can happen

It may come as a shock, but a recent study of college women found that more than 65% of respondents have faced some form of sexual harassment. Awareness is key, so read our chapter and be prepared in case you, too, ever have to deal with this unfortunate reality.

Take a self-defense class

This is a great way to prepare yourself for *anything* that can happen on campus or in your community. Look for these classes on-campus first; your instructors will most likely spend some time talking about your campus specifically—important information that can help you become better aware of your surroundings.

Looking for more great advice? Head to UniversityChic.com and look for "U Chic Picks!" for our fav resources and websites—they come highly recommended from our guide's contributors and editors. Be sure to leave your suggestions as well!

CHAPTER 10

Money Matters

Living on a budget, hunting for an apartment, staying on top of credit card bills: these are just a few of the "real world" (well, sort of real world) responsibilities and experiences that you'll face as an independent woman in college. On the surface, they don't sound like much fun. However, you'll find that there is something to be said about taking charge of your life. You'll develop a sense of pride, and more than anything, these good self-management habits will last a lifetime. When it comes down to it, this is definitely a chapter that you do not want to skip. So read on to get inspired with advice from other college women who discovered their inner diva by successfully pursuing the independent life.

avoiding the credit card black hole

Nisha Chittal, University of Illinois – Urbana-Champaign

About a year ago, I was an inexperienced freshman, gearing up for a spring-break trip to Morocco and Spain. I had never been to either of these countries before and was excited beyond belief to experience a new culture. The only problem? I had no money. I had borrowed hundreds of dollars already from my parents to pay for my flights and some hotel expenses, and they were refusing to loan me another cent. As the trip got closer, I started getting more desperate. I had a job, but $7.50 an hour wasn't going to be enough to cover my expenses. In complete desperation, I even tried to sell plasma but was told—much to my disappointment—that my veins were too small for them to take blood and I would not be able to sell my plasma! That's really bad.

At this point, it looked like I would be surviving on bread and water in Spain unless I came up with a better solution. So, I did what any utterly broke college student would do in my situation: I applied for a credit card, and a student card at that! It was one of the easiest application processes I had ever been through—a rushed process, in fact! However, the day it arrived, I had a strange sense of foreboding as I opened up the congratulatory letter from Citicards. For years, I had heard all the warnings of how I should be careful with credit cards. But I quickly forgot the nagging feelings of doubt as I prepared for my trip to exotic lands.

Well, the trip was incredible; I managed to make it out with only a hundred dollars in credit card debt, and my job helped me to pay it off quickly. However, most young women are not as fortunate when it comes to credit card debt. Just a few days ago I watched a 21-year-old woman on a daytime talk show confess to having $50,000 in credit card debt just from shopping and had previously had *another* $50,000 in debt that her mother had already paid off!

As a college student, you will face the same credit challenges that I did before my trip abroad, and maybe some of you have even experienced this in high school. In addition to expensive spring break trips to paradise, you'll worry about having enough money to pay for a variety of bills, food, clothes, and those nights out with your friends. To top it off, the credit card companies will go out of their way to make it easy for you to swipe your way into debt. Their typical sales tactic? Offering a student version of a card that has good interest rates and a high credit limit.

With all this temptation to get one and spend, is it realistic to believe that you can beat the credit card debt trap? And besides, how can you beat the trap when there are so many people that haven't?

To some extent, the problem lies in the fact that credit cards are a way of life. Used wisely, they can be a useful tool to have and help you manage your money. They also help you build good credit that can help years down the road when applying for a mortgage, but only if you pay your bills on time and in full. Rather than give up and resign yourself to a life of bad credit, use these strategies to prevent yourself from ending up like the countless thirty-something women still paying off the thousands of dollars of credit card debt they racked up during their teens and twenties.

CHOOSING WISELY

If you're going to take the plunge and get a credit card, make sure you do your research first. And limit yourself to one card at a time rather than opening several different ones; it will be easier to keep track of and pay one bill a month.

U Chic Tip!

Credit card companies don't want you to pay your bill electronically because they will never get to charge you late fees or raise your interest rate when you miss a payment. One of their tricks is to initially give you a low interest rate, and then raise it through the roof as soon as you're late on a payment.

When doing your research, pay attention to interest rates before signing a contract; credit card companies are not afraid to take advantage of students who don't read the fine print on their contract. Three of the features that credit card companies use most often to entrap students are low credit limits, low-income requirements (if any), and high interest rates. A Bankrate.com survey found that the average interest rate on a student credit card is 17.51%—ouch! Try aiming for a rate lower than 8%. For more info on common credit card terminology, visit the Adventures in Education website: www.aie.org.

No matter what, don't let yourself get tricked into signing up for a card advertising "low student rates"; make sure to read the fine print very carefully and make sure that low means low.

Really, using a credit card is no different than walking into a bank and taking out a loan for "entertainment expenses." It is way better to only use a debit card, which draws money automatically from your bank account, so you will never pile up any debt for items you didn't have the cash to buy.

GET A LOW LIMIT

Most reputable creditors will offer only very low credit limits to students who have little or no income and little or no established credit history. This is usually a good thing, since it acts as a built-in check to keep your spending under control. However, not all creditors are this kind; some are willing to give you credit limits of thousands of dollars. My first credit card, which I still have today, gave me a $4,000 credit limit from the day I signed up. Thankfully, I have never racked up more than a few hundred dollars at a time and have been able to pay off the balance each month, preventing a buildup of debt. But in retrospect, being handed that $4,000 credit limit as a naïve, inexperienced freshman was a potential recipe for disaster!

PAY IT OFF EVERY MONTH—ON TIME

One of the most important pieces of advice about credit cards goes without saying: pay off the balance in full every month before the due date or try to pay off more than the minimum payment if not the full balance. You have the option to pay late, but you'll also face penalties like finance fees ($30 a pop!) and the potential that the card company will raise your interest rate.

PAY YOUR BILL ELECTRONICALLY

The credit card companies make a lot of money off of late fees, and off of raising your interest rate when your payment is late. The best way to avoid this is to set up "automatic payment" from your bank account, so you will never be late with a payment.

WHAT TO WATCH OUT FOR

Credit card statements will offer to let you pay a minimum each month, which is just a small portion of the total bill—sometimes around $20 to $50. If you're only paying the minimum, interest will accrue on whatever part of the balance rolls over to the next month and you may only be paying on the interest and not the original amount that was charged. The result? You actually end up paying the credit card company to hold your debt for you. Credit card companies are making enough; they don't need any additional help!

BUILD UP GOOD CREDIT

By paying off your bills in full each month on time, you will begin to establish a good credit history. This is extremely important in life—having a good credit history allows you to make large purchases like a house or a car, take out a loan, open certain types of bank accounts, and even apply for certain jobs. While it may seem boring and unnecessary to worry about now, women who neglected their credit scores while in college have regretted it for the rest of their lives when they weren't able to get a house, a car, or go on the vacation of their dreams! Sure, the "live in the moment" strategy seems great today, but you'll be sorry tomorrow.

TRY PAYING IN CASH OR WITH YOUR DEBIT CARD

Once that credit card is in your wallet, sometimes it's just difficult to resist the temptation to use it. So many things are available to you now! It's tempting when walking through the mall, or even down a shop-lined street off campus, to stop by and pick something up and come up with all kinds of reasons to justify it to yourself. (I just aced my exam! Or I just bombed my exam and need to treat myself!)

As you already know, college is a drain on your finances. You can work a part-time job for 30 hours a week and still feel like you don't have enough money to keep up with your rich friends or sorority sisters. But don't let credit cards get the best of you. Though it may seem hard right now to have an outdated wardrobe or have to skip your spring break with your friends (believe me, I know!) it's not worth getting drowned in debt that will haunt you for the rest of your life and make it difficult for you to buy a home or a car one day. If you're going to use credit cards, think smart and only buy what you can pay off at the end of the month. Don't let your credit cards control your life!

living fabulously on a budget

Lativia Jones Bolarinwa, University of North Carolina—Chapel Hill

*I*f you haven't done so already, you'll soon be making the clichéd reference to yourself as a poor college student. I will be the first to admit that college can be tough at times—having to worry about grades, extracurriculars, working for low pay—all while trying to be trendy and up on the latest iPhone or other gadget that all our friends seem to have these days. Well, it's time for us to stop feeling sorry for ourselves for being financially challenged and start living fabulously despite our limited monetary possessions. Living the fabulous life on a budget is all about budgeting for *your* life, not your best friend's, not your parents', and definitely not those brats' on *My Super Sweet 16* (turn off your TV, now!).

THE B WORD: BUDGET

The first part in achieving this fabulous life is making a fabulous budget. Start your "fabulous financial budget" by recording all of your monthly expenses and due dates and then compare that to your projected monthly income. When writing down your expenses also include things that are bought on a regular basis like gas, groceries, etc. Once you have your monthly budget set, limit your weekly expenses to whatever you have left over after taking into account your monthly financial goals.

If one of your goals is to save money, consider your monthly savings goals as part of your monthly expenses, and don't dip into your savings when spending your weekly allowance. One trick that can help (because we all have those days when an extra grande mocha with whip would solve everything) is what I call being "blind" to the savings—having money automatically moved into you savings account each pay period, whether each week or month. Sometimes it's easier to save if it's done automatically for you at regular intervals.

Now, if your monthly expenses are greater than what you make each month, you're a bit further behind in staying on a budget. However, no matter how far you may be behind in being financially responsible, it's never too late to get organized and headed in the right direction.

Last piece of advice: don't forget that budgeting has to be more than just a monthly occurrence. You must think about your budget on a daily and weekly basis.

WAYS TO CUT COSTS

If there is one thing that can't be emphasized enough it is to always pay your bills on time to avoid those unnecessary late fees and other charges. If you find that you are having trouble keeping up on your payments, contact your credit card company(s) or other creditors to work out a payment plan. These entities are willing to work with you, but you have to make the effort to stay in touch with them and let them know about your situation. When it comes to your credit cards, the obvious way to keep your fabulous financial budget is to not bite off more than you can chew and keep your debt down. If possible, make sure you pay your cards completely off and on time and only buy things that you know you can actually afford.

Also, if your annual percentage rate on your credit card is high and you're carrying a balance every month, it never hurts to call your credit card company and ask for a lower interest rate. To get them to deal, threaten to switch card companies if they will not give you a lower rate. Despite what you may have heard, credit card companies really do work with their customers and, more often than not, will come up with ways to help you pay your bills more easily.

Another place that you can easily cut costs is grocery shopping. Always make a list before you go, and follow the old saying "Never go to the grocery store hungry." When you're shopping on an empty stomach, everything looks appealing and you'll end up buying things that you don't need. The same thing happens when you shop without a list; having a list to follow when you grocery shop helps you focus on buying the things you need and helps prevent useless spending each month.

FABULOUS BUDGET-SAVERS

Now we can chat about the fun part of living fabulously on a budget—finding ways to cut corners and spend less money while still being utterly fabulous. You know how sugar gives you a little rush when the chemical dopamine gets released in your brain boosting your happiness level. The same thing can happen when you find great ways to save money! I call these happiness boosters "budget-savers." They can help you save a little or even a lot of money each day, week, and month.

One big budget-saver for me is investing in sandwich-sized storage bags and filling them each morning with snacks like almonds, Cheez-its, Chex Mix, or other little snacks to eat during the day to satiate my hunger. It prevents me from buying snacks from those overpriced student stores on campus. Also by having a little snack throughout the day, I can spend less money on lunch because I'm not as hungry.

Another great budget-saver for me has been to learn how to do a lot of things for myself rather than having to pay someone else to do them, like cutting or coloring my hair, basic manicures and pedicures, and waxing. The list goes on. You end up saving so much more money in the long run while learning a useful skill.

U Chic Tip! Great Budget-Savers for Chic College Chicks

- **Group your errands.** Make a to-do list of any errands you need to run in a similar part of town for one day. By running all your errands while you're already out and about, you can often save money on gas. Usually, I'll run all my errands during the week after work, so I don't have to travel anywhere on the weekends.

- **Take the bus.** Many college towns have buses to help get students around. If you live on a bus line, try taking the bus to class once or twice a week rather than driving.

- **Search the newspaper for savings.** No, coupon clipping and searching the sale pages of newspapers aren't just for your grandmother. There is actually some good sale information in there that could be useful for a college chick on a budget

- **Invest in a wholesale store membership.** BJ's, Costco, Sam's Club—whatever it is—bite the bullet and buy a membership. Or split the cost with a roommate(s) or friend(s). Buying in bulk can help you save a lot in the long run.

- **Learn to cook.** Besides saving money, you'll be popular. Who doesn't like having a friend who can cook?

TREAT YOURSELF

What's a fabulous budget without the fabulous part? The most important part of maintaining a great budget, without going totally insane, is treating yourself with little things every now and then so the undeniable urge to splurge won't build. For instance, small treats like a movie or a magazine once a week or a new pair of shoes or purse at the end of the month should keep you satisfied to resist that dreadful urge.

BE THRIFTY!

Shopping at thrift stores or heading for the sales racks is a great way to save money while still being able to shop. Learn some basic sewing skills so that you can buy that ultra cute dress with the missing button for half-off and fix the button later. Try making thrift store or sale rack shopping a special outing with your friends on a regular basis. Who's going to resist the opportunity to shop *and* save money?

There are so many ways to live fabulously while being on a budget. By mapping out your expenses and financial goals, finding budget-savers, and treating yourself every now and then, you'll not only be living fabulously on a budget in college, but you'll be living a fabulous life as well!

U Chic Essentials—Money Matters

Embrace your independence

You're in college, on your own now, and for most readers this is the first time in your life that you're in charge! Embrace this independence by establishing good money management skills, and you'll be setting yourself up for success not only in college but beyond.

Start a budget

The key to financial success is having a budget in place that is easy to follow. By knowing what your limits are ahead of time, you are more likely to not overspend. We know it's hard, but it will pay off in the end.

Cash only

When you're out having fun with your friends on a Friday night, you're less likely to want to stick to that budget that we discussed above. To prevent you from buying and drinking one too many, take a limited amount of cash with you. Your more rational self will thank you later!

You can even set this aside for your spring break trip.

Looking for more great advice? Head to www.UniversityChic.com and look for "U Chic Picks!" for our fav resources and websites—they come highly recommended from our guide's contributors and editors. Be sure to leave your suggestions as well!

CHAPTER 11

The College Perks

ollege tuition is expensive these days. Sometimes you have to wonder where all of this money is going. Well, if you already are spending the cash on attending college, why not try to maximize all your opportunities while you're there—a surefire way to get a bang out of every buck going into your college's pockets. From finding internships to networking and reaching out to alumni to studying abroad, your school has a range of services, or as we like to call them, "college perks," set up to help you find your path in school and life. So what are you waiting for? Read on to learn about all the opportunities that await you in college.

secrets for landing that hot job or internship

Pamela O'Leary, University of California–Berkeley

*I*f there is one piece of advice I have to pass along it would have to be that internships are a must-do during college. They help you figure out your interests and can even land you a job right out of college—which is a key reason you're in school, anyways. I have many friends who worked at the State Department, Department of Homeland Security, and Congress right after college because they impressed their bosses during their internships and utilized the connections they made. Internships are simply the best way for you to gain professional experience while still an undergraduate. Bottom line: you really need to check out and take advantage of these opportunities.

BUT WHERE DO I BEGIN?

The process of finding an internship can potentially be daunting, but above anything else you must keep a positive attitude through the *entire* process, from rejection to rejection to finally an offer. Be excited by all the possibilities! Be open to exploring different areas. It is just as important to know what you don't want to do as it is to know what you do want to do.

Although you may not realize it, you already have access to a treasure chest of resources that can help you snag that hot internship opportunity. A good first step would be to drop by your university's career center. You can talk to a career counselor or review the school's database to see if your university has any established relationships with certain programs. Some may even keep satisfaction surveys from students who previously completed the same internship—another great way to figure out which internship is right for you. The counselors can also provide feedback on your résumé and cover letter.

In addition to the career center, don't be afraid to ask your professor, academic advisor, or teaching assistant if they have any recommendations. They may be able to directly connect you to an organization. If you haven't heard it already, connections really do matter!

U Chic Tip!

Sometimes an internship may sound great on paper, but the actual experience may be less-than-stellar thanks to a poorly managed internship program. How to avoid this? Track down people who have previously done the internship, and check for satisfaction surveys in your university's career center to help you better understand your options.

For those looking for advice for specific internships, I've provided some tips for you below.

Wanting to work at a not-for-profit?

Looking for nonprofit work experience? You're in luck. There are many good websites such as Idealist.org that focus on posting internships and jobs, so check them out regularly and get on their mailing lists. In the nonprofit world, internships are like entry-level positions that often lead to a job afterward. But be prepared to work for free; it's a short-term sacrifice that can eventually land you a paid position.

For the corporate-minded

Want to work for an investment bank or a *Fortune* 500 company? As advised above, go to your college's career center and find out in advance about opportunities such as on-campus recruitment and local career fairs, company campus visits, and other unique programs they may have for the corporate-minded. Ask your relevant professors or mentors about potential opportunities. Take the initiative to thoroughly research the company by checking out their career or internship websites. Many companies have college recruitment programs and provide a lot of detail online to give you a sense of the corporate culture and opportunities for advancement. The company likely has established internship programs with set deadlines for which you will need to plan ahead to meet.

Interested in the government?

If you are interested in politics, you should definitely consider interning in Washington DC, whether on Capitol Hill, a think tank, or a nonprofit organization. Many colleges have established programs that will guide you through the process of finding an internship and may even help you find housing. For example, the Public Leadership Education Network (PLEN) is a national organization whose sole mission is preparing women for public leadership (www.plen.org). Participating in a program like PLEN can be an added credential that can help get you an internship.

Politics is all about networking and connections, so definitely take advantage of any personal connections you may have (family connections, professors' connections, alumni networks, etc.). For example, if you want to intern on the Hill, you should apply to multiple offices and not just those from your home state, even though you may have a better chance at getting one of these coveted spots from your home state. When applying to the Hill, prepare a succinct one-page résumé and make sure you comprehensively research the office before you interview. Ideally, it's preferable that you intern full-time rather than part-time, so you gain a better understanding of how things run day-to-day and your organization or institution gets to know you better (think future letters of recommendation).

U Chic Tip!

If you are aware that a particular congresswoman or congressional representative is interested in an issue that you are passionate about, consider applying to their office. In your cover letter, explain how you're passionate about the issue and include any specific experiences you've had that show this passion. For instance, did you organize a campus demonstration? Tell them and put this in your résumé, detailing the success you had in organizing a group of people.

For the budding young journalist or media maven

If you're considering a job in the media, there is no better time to start than now. And with the Internet, you can start as soon as you finish reading this chapter. Pick a topic that you love, and start a blog. Blog as often as you can (daily is most preferable to build a following), and you soon may be considered an expert on the particular topic you chose. As for other relevant experience, write for your college paper or even local newspaper during school. If you're interested in PR or marketing, join your campus organization for these careers, like the Public Relations Student Society of America (PRSSA; www.prssa.org) or the Society of Professional Journalists (www.spj. org), and aim to become a leader in the organization. These groups are a fantastic way to get to know the leaders in your industry through campus discussions, projects, and their close affiliation with their large parent organization. If these organizations do not have a chapter on campus, consider starting one! Nothing shows more initiative than getting a group off the ground and running on your own. When you are applying for internships in the field, be sure to call attention to your blog, campus paper clippings, and your involvement in campus organizations.

Dreaming of a job in medicine?

Medical school admissions offices like to see that you have clinical experience and are seriously interested in the profession. Volunteer in a hospital or clinic or become an Emergency Medical Technician (EMT). Participating in undergraduate research is another great way to prepare for medical school. See if your school has an established undergraduate research or independent study program. If such a program does not yet exist, feel free to approach professors whose work you are interested in. Think of a new project idea that you could collaborate on with them or think of a way you can assist them with a current project. Nothing shows more interest in medicine (well, a top grade in Organic Chemistry doesn't hurt) than conducting outside research and even getting it published in a medical or scientific journal.

No clue what you're interested in?

That's fine! College is about taking your time to figure yourself out and discover your likes and dislikes. Apply for an internship in an area that you are interested in. Who knows, you could love it or hate it, but you'll never know your preferences unless you explore different areas.

BE PROACTIVE!

The Internet is your best friend. So love it and use it! If you are interested in a certain organization, check out their website, particularly the "About Us" section. This is where they usually state if they have current internship vacancies or regular internship application periods. Don't be afraid to call the organization and ask if there is a particular person you can address your application to. However, if the posting says "no calls" be respectful of that and don't call. Subscribe to as many listservs of organizations as you can, and you'll soon be amazed by all the opportunities you can randomly find out about from being on a listserv.

It's All about the Small Stuff

Harmony Haveman, Pacific Lutheran University

Internships will be your ticket to a job at the end of senior year when all of your friends are frantically searching for any job they can find. I had the most incredible opportunity to do three internships abroad thanks to networking and using the connections I had made along the way. I was able to intern at CNN International in London, MGM Television in London, and I also did an internship with the United Nations in Geneva, Switzerland. These experiences changed my life and paved the way for my career.

So how did I swing these fantastic opportunities? *It's all about the small stuff.* I went to every event that had anything to do with journalism. I was fortunate to get the internship at CNN International in London thanks to attending one of the many seminars about journalism at my university. It took being one of just a handful of college students to show up at an event to get my name out there. It was there I met someone who worked for CNN. Because I was only one of a few students there I had a great opportunity to talk about my future with this professional. After meeting with me and learning about my passion for journalism and my future, she said she'd help me get an internship at CNN in London. Those little connections make all the difference in the real world. I am a firm believer that it's a lot about who you know and even more about how to treat people.

TIMING AND FOLLOW-UP

Ideally, the goal is to plan ahead and apply to internships before the deadline. However, if you're like most of us, you get busy and may end up missing a deadline for an internship that you would have loved to have. Don't be afraid to just go ahead and apply even if it's close or the deadline has passed. Write in your cover letter that you are aware the deadline has passed, but you are still interested and available (this works especially well if you live near the organization). For example, toward the end of the spring semester, I finally decided I wanted to intern somewhere in San Francisco during the summer. I sent my résumé to many nonprofit organizations, even if they were not advertising an open position. I finally received a response from Greenpeace and interned there for the summer.

THE WAITING GAME

Don't be shy when going after something you want. Follow-up is a door-opening technique that can land you that great internship or job. If a decent amount of time has passed (use your judgment), it's definitely OK (actually, more like mandatory) to make a follow-up email or phone call. Keep it simple, "On April 10, I sent you my application for the summer internship. I am still interested in the position and would like to please check the status of my application."

This worked for me when I landed a graduate internship at the United Nations. I applied for a summer internship and received an email from the UN saying that my application was still under consideration but they recommended that I apply again for a fall internship. So I applied again for the fall session but soon received a similar email. This time, I responded directly to this email, asking about the status of my application. I was told that the department I originally applied to no longer accepted applications, but if I was able to move to New York in the next few weeks, they would forward my information to other departments. Since I had good girlfriends from college whom I could indefinitely crash with, I was able to move from Los Angeles to New York immediately. So I asked them to please forward my information, and I quickly received a phone interview and an internship offer. I sent the follow-up email, and within a month, my dream came true of finally interning at the UN. The point of this story? Be persistent and your dreams will come true!

DON'T PUT ALL YOUR EGGS IN ONE BASKET

Don't be too emotionally attached to a single application; have faith that in the end it will all work out for the best. I applied to Teach for America twice, the first time during my senior year and then a year later when I was in graduate school. I was rejected both times. The first time I made it to the final stage of an interview; I thought it went really well, but I was not accepted into the program. I applied again a year later and was not even given a phone interview. Both times I got rejected I felt really bad about myself. My partner was accepted to Teach for America during our senior year. I hate to admit it, but initially I was really jealous. How silly was I! You should never compare yourself to anyone else! Everyone has a different life path. Reflecting back, I realized all the amazing things I have been able to do during the two years I would have potentially been in Teach for America. I volunteered in Kenya, lived in Egypt, got a master's degree, interned at the United Nations, and did a fellowship in the United States Congress. In the end, it all really worked out, and as much as I wanted to do Teach for America during the times I applied, I truly believe things worked out for a reason.

APPLY, APPLY, APPLY!

Put yourself out there to the universe! People fear rejection, and this can prevent them from applying for multiple opportunities. One friend applied for two internships and got one offer. Another friend applied for ten and got only three offers. That's a lower success rate, but she has three times as many opportunities as my other friend—3 versus 1.

Last piece of advice: keep your hopes up! Honestly, ever since my senior year of college, every week (if not every day!) I apply to different opportunities. I have a solid résumé and cover letter (which I adapt to each posting) that I am able to send out as soon as I learn of opportunities. The more you put yourself out there, the more chances you have of things working out. Not applying is the only sure way of *not* landing that great job or internship.

using summers wisely

Olga Belogolova, Boston University

*I*t's that time of year when all of your exams have finished and this massive ray of sunshine is finding its way through your bedroom window. You reluctantly open your eyes, curl up in the corner of your bed, grab the blanket, and wonder what Mom's made for breakfast as you slowly roll your way out of bed and wander over to the bathroom to brush your teeth. You brush away diligently as you look at the clock hanging on the opposite wall.

What?

Noon.

No way.

You squint again thinking that maybe your eyes haven't fully opened yet.

Noon.

Seriously? Then you look at yourself in the mirror and think. What am I doing with my life?

WHAT TO DO WITH THE SUMMER

Summertime for a college student can mean one of two things:

Sleeping and being a couch bum

This is probably not your best option. As much as it is tempting and easy to stay put, let's be honest. You will get bored. You will regret it. And you have so much more that you can do with your time.

Getting up off that comfy couch and heading to work

Although you are supposed to be getting an education in the classroom, one of the most valuable educations you can get is through a summer job. In fact, here's some shocking news: your summer job might be the only educational experience you'll need before graduation, as it will be teaching you more about something you will actually be *doing* when you graduate. Where else can you get this hands-on, practical experience?

If you're like most kids at the end of their teenage years and heading into their twenties, you have absolutely no clue what you want to do with your life. So, how does a summer job cure that? And what's the point of having a job if you don't know what job you want?

THE SIMPLE MATTER OF MONEY

Loans don't pay for themselves and neither do those movie tickets or those fancy-schmancy cocktails. There is only so long you can hold on to that cash that your grandparents gave you for Hanukkah or Christmas. Sooner or later, you won't be able to puppy-face your way into some extra money for your bank account and even if you could, do you really want to? One of the rewarding things of having your own money is that it makes you independent. You are your own person and you are one step closer to being a responsible adult. OK, maybe the word "responsible" doesn't make it sound *that* appealing, but trust me, it is. If you are actually going to dive into that world of responsibility, then why not use your summer wisely and get a job that not only makes you money, but also opens up opportunities for your future in a field you actually want to work in.

HAVING SUMMER JOBS IS KIND OF LIKE DATING

Thanks to this wonderful invention called an internship (or part-time job), you get to essentially date different jobs. You let the man (aka, internship) take you out for a drink or dinner and it's on him; and maybe you realize that perhaps he wasn't what you wanted. No worries; you're only there for a few more weeks. Or maybe you go out on that first date and realize that you don't know enough about him, so you plan for round two—another summer at the same place. Best-case scenario: you realize you really do like him and then not only have you gotten a nice drink or dinner, but you enjoyed it, too, and you are glad you went out and learned something about this guy. This might be the start of a lifelong relationship.

Bottom line: we, as students today, are very lucky. We don't have to just get thrown into any job and stick with it forever like our parents or grandparents did. Thanks to internships and summer jobs, we get a taste of what life is like in the real world, getting a teensy-weensy bit closer to that elusive dream of actually getting paid to do something we love to do. Everybody wants it. Hardly anybody gets it. Fact of life.

YOU'VE DECIDED TO DO SOMETHING PRODUCTIVE THIS SUMMER, WHAT NEXT?

So once you've peeled yourself off that couch and made the decision to use that summer wisely…what's next? Where to go?

Finding a summer job starts way before the summer sun shows itself in the sky. Most summer jobs and internships start recruiting for positions as early as the autumn leaves turn slightly orangey-yellow. So start looking early. It will pay off with a better opportunity in the end—guaranteed.

Career fairs

Most colleges have career centers where you can find everything ranging from résumé help to career fairs and even summer internship recruiting. So step number one: find your college career center in person or online at their website and make an appointment. Go in and tell them that you've never made a résumé before and you're completely lost or—to be ahead of the game—go in with that résumé you've been hammering away at and ask them what they think.

Talk up alumni

Other useful college resources are the very people who used to be you—the alumni. Once upon a time, all those bosses and scary recruiters used to be college students just like you. They know finding a job is hard and, maybe even more importantly, they know you are smart. You go to the same school they went to! They know you will work hard and if you prove your commitment, they might even help you find a job.

The importance of persistence

Now, if you know what job you want, be annoying. Honestly! Just don't call every day, especially when on the job description they ask you not to. Find the place that you want to work at and email them or give them a call. Ask them if they are looking for interns or someone to help out or just ask for some advice about what kind of person they would want or what kind of internships you should take on before you apply for a job there. They might not reply, but if they do, you will have some valuable advice for your future or maybe even a job.

In addition, you can find that famous author or lab specialist you've been dreaming to ask for advice. Contact them. They are only human, and so are you. The worst thing that will happen is they won't answer. But if they do, it is really quite exciting.

Here's a basic summary on talking to alums or strangers who have your dream job: In the best-case scenario, you have contacted someone in the business that you want to be in and they tell you what kind of qualifications they think you would need and advise you on a good starting point. In the best-case, magical, and most amazingly amazing scenario, you get a job out of it.

Where else can you get a job?

Ask around. As much as we don't want to admit it, it's always about who you know. Ask your parents, ask your parents' friends, ask your friends' parents. Ask your professor. *Ask away.* Someone, somewhere must have an opening for the summer, and would certainly love to have an eager college student who knows how to use a computer better than some of the people in the office do. They may even like the fact you "get" the whole social-networking thing. Most companies today are interested in how they, too, can use Facebook to do better business. Make it known that you're an expert!

WHAT TO DO ONCE YOU GET THE JOB

Make sure to get to know the people at your office. Everyone around you can either be someone to learn from or a possible future contact for a job or recommendation. If you make the right impression and show that you are willing to learn, they will want to help you with your career and future.

Go to any of the lunches or dinners they have. Not only will you get a free meal out of it, but you will also gain a better relationship with a boss that you might want to write you a recommendation or offer you another internship or even a full-time job.

As we've already seen and admitted, it really is about who you know. The girl whose desk is next to yours might end up knowing a girl whose brother's girlfriend's mom works at your dream job and if you become good friends, she just might be that person who you turn to for next summer's job.

Learn as much as you can. Always ask for more work or more responsibility. Use the fact that you are smart and skilled with computers and do twice as much work as they expect you to do. That way, when you leave at the end of the summer, they will realize just how indispensable you are and that they just want you back as soon as you finish college. Even if you don't particularly want to have that job again, chances are that your résumé can use the boost of those new skills you picked up over the summer. Impress your bosses and coworkers. Show them that you are worth a stellar review or even a full-time job.

Last piece of advice? Meet up with your good friends—new and old. Let them ground you. Let them be there for you. Have a good time. Live.

the ins and outs of networking

Pamela O'Leary, University of California–Berkeley

You probably have heard it many times before: networking can be the key to landing your dream internship or job. As a college student, worries about your future job can seem eons away. They're not. In today's work world, networking is the name of the game—even in college. It's incredibly important to your success and advancement in the workforce.

Did You Know?

Between 50–75% of people found their last job through networking, and so can you! People will be especially impressed and receptive when college students take initiative and reach out to them.

As a college student, you have tremendous access to resources and many different kinds of networking opportunities such as professors, campus lectures, career fairs, internships, student organizations, etc. Before you know it, graduation will be here, so you need to take advantage of these opportunities now! Simply put, networking is about connecting with people, knowing how to talk to them, and later utilizing those connections.

U Chic Tip!

Before you begin heading out to networking events, try making a list of your priorities. This will help focus your efforts when you begin making those all-important connections. Ask yourself…

1. What organizations or events are related to your interests, but you have not yet pursued?

2. What dreams do you have that you've always wanted to make a reality?

3. What are your strongest skills that you can share with others?

4. What skills would you like to improve, and who could help you develop them?

5. How can you take more initiative in networking (maybe going to an event by yourself, checking out a new group, asking a friend to introduce you to someone, etc.)?

WHERE TO START

Networking can take place in person and (even more so these days) online. So, if you are on Facebook or MySpace, then you are already networking! Also, another important thing to note is that networking can be done with anyone around you at any time, not just in professional settings. You can network with your roommates, people who live in your residence hall, classmates, coworkers, friends of friends, professors, supervisors, members of clubs you are in, etc. I feel that I gained significant networking skills through recruitment for my sorority. So joining student organizations is a great way to hone your networking skills. If you are at a lecture on a topic you are very interested in, approach the speakers afterward and introduce yourself. Try to even get their email address for future questions. They could end up being a mentor. Also, it's important to build relationships with your professors and teaching assistants, as they, too, can help connect you with potential employers. So don't be shy. Visit them during their office hours so they can get to know you. These relationships are crucial to getting a good letter of recommendation when you apply to all those exciting internships.

PRACTICE MAKES PERFECT

Like anything in life, networking may be awkward at first, but know that your skills will grow with practice. If you are attending a networking event, first and foremost, have confidence and enjoy yourself. Don't think of it as "I am networking." This will make you nervous. Approach the event as if it's a new opportunity to meet new people. Most of all, don't doubt yourself; you are awesome, so act like it—*smile!* Have welcoming body language—make eye contact, don't fold your arms, and give a pleasant greeting with a firm handshake. Bottom line: be your confident self.

When networking, you need to take initiative. Sitting in a corner alone or clinging to your friends won't expand your horizons. Go ahead, approach others, and introduce yourself. A great icebreaker can be something as simple as "Oh I like your bag…where did you get it?"

Have a purpose to your networking—a concrete goal. For example, let's say you are interested in summer internship opportunities; this narrows the conversation and makes it less awkward. Ask open-ended questions rather than questions that evoke a simple yes/no response. Also, recognize that networking is just as much about how you can help them as they can help you. Without even knowing it, you have something of value to them. Keep talking; you'll never know what you'll discover. It's like the idea of "to have a friend, be a friend."

U Chic Tip!

Networking is a two-way street. It's about giving and taking. Once you put yourself out there and help someone out, it will come back to you twofold in ways you could not imagine. Case in point, I was able to contribute chapters in this book because of networking.

And really try to build rapport. People love to talk about themselves. Let the other person talk and listen intently to what they have to say (show this with positive body language). When the conversation ends, repeat their name when you leave: "It was great meeting you, Maria." People like to hear their name and will be impressed you remembered it.

HOW DO I UTILIZE THIS CONNECTION LATER?

Make up some business cards so the people you meet can contact you later. This is probably the most important thing you should do in advance of any major networking events, and they don't have to be anything fancy. Your name, contact info, major area of study, expected graduation date, and school should appear on the card. Do you have an online résumé? Put the link on your card too! You'll also want to be collecting theirs, or at least writing down their name and some form of contact information to get in touch with them later. Except for shipping and handling, you can get business cards made for free at www.VistaPrint.com or www. MOO.com. After you make a connection, write down some details about the person on the back of their card or wherever you record their contact info so you can remember details about them later.

The most important piece of advice? The great connection you just made does not go anywhere unless you follow up, and the sooner the better. Soon after you met them, within a day ideally, send them a quick email. Remind them who you are and where you met. Thank them for taking the time to talk with you. End with an action item of how to build your connection with them, such as getting coffee together. However, if you don't necessarily want to meet them soon to discuss a certain issue, then don't feel that you are obligated to do so. For example, if the person you met was a peer, you can add them as a new Facebook or MySpace friend, and later build the connection through those online social networking tools.

Sample follow-up email:

Hi Maria,

It was great meeting you at the UC–Berkeley environmental career fair. Thanks for talking with me about summer opportunities with the National Park Service. I am very interested in learning more about your career as a research scientist. Please let me know if you are available for coffee sometime next week.

Thank you,
Sunitha

INFORMATIONAL INTERVIEWS

Believe it or not, you are scheduled for an informational interview with Maria and you got one! Richard Nelson Bolles, author of the career guide *What Color Is Your Parachute?*, describes the informational interview process as "trying on jobs to see if they fit you."

Did You Know?

Studies estimate that 1 out of every 200 to 1,500 résumés result in a job offer. However, 1 out of every 12 informational interviews results in a job offer. Truly, informational interviews are a great tool in landing your dream job!

Informational interviews are a first step to introduce yourself to an organization you'd like to work for in the near future, so be prepared to make a strong first impression. Everyone loves to meet with students, so don't be afraid to try to contact people you have never met before. For instance, you can call an organization and ask for someone by job title or search through professional organizations. Assure them that the purpose of your inquiry is to learn more about the employer and occupation rather than to haggle them for an actual job. Informational interviews are separate from you applying for a job, so don't make this the time you ask them for a job. Make sure to do significant research on the background of the organization and the person you are going to meet.

Since you requested this interview, you will be the one asking the questions. Make a list of questions you plan on asking. Dress appropriately, bring copies of your résumé, and be prepared to take notes. Listen intently to the person to fully take advantage of the knowledge they are sharing. At the end, kindly ask if they can give you referrals of other people in the industry that would be willing to meet with you. Make sure you send the person you met a thank-you note shortly after the interview.

The more people you meet, the more chances you have of making successful connections. Since you're investing in yourself and reading this book, you are already on your way to being a networking queen. Go out there, show the world how amazing you are, and meet tons of amazing new friends and colleagues! That's what college is all about.

when to go abroad

Kathryn Lewis, University of North Carolina–Chapel Hill

One of the greatest perks you have these days as a college student is the opportunity to study abroad. And why wouldn't you? It almost seems like a requirement that you study abroad at some point during your time in college. What a great requirement! Who wouldn't want to study in some exotic place like Italy, Japan, or even somewhere in Africa? The decision to study abroad is the easy one to make. It's deciding *when* to study abroad that may keep you up at night.

The key to making this decision is to go when you are ready. What do I mean when I say *ready*? Ready means that you are academically, socially, and financially prepared for this adventure of a lifetime. So here's how you can get prepared.

GETTING ACADEMICALLY READY

Before you study abroad, I highly recommend that you first decide on your major. Some study-abroad applications will even ask you how you will use time abroad to gain credits toward your major. On top of that, several programs are actually targeted to specific majors, making it an added bonus to know your major before heading abroad. Think about it: there's nothing more relevant and fulfilling than going on an archeological dig in Greece if you're an archeology or anthropology major.

After deciding on a major, try to complete at least one semester of major coursework. This may be difficult for those of you who have been itching to take your first-ever tango class in a bar in Buenos Aires. I completely understand this urge. But a semester of class is really the only way to make sure that you still want to pursue the major. After all, if you decide to change majors, you may need to stick around the good old USA for an extra semester—the one you would have spent abroad—in order to graduate on time.

Which year makes the most sense?

Deciding when to go abroad is a very personal decision, so I can't say what is right for you. From my experience, sophomore or junior year are more popular years to head to foreign lands, probably because most college students are more settled and ready for the experience of living abroad. Indeed, when I was in Florence, Italy, a large percentage of the students I met abroad were also juniors. As a freshman in college, you are still discovering your passions—who you really are. Going abroad during your first year may prevent you from making this all-important discovery. True, I did meet one freshman abroad, and from all appearances (dancing on tabletops at the local hot spots!) she was enjoying herself. But I think the important thing to understand is that college is your first opportunity to get a taste of independence. It is usually best to get comfortable in one new situation before deciding to put yourself in another one that involves a different culture and probably a different language.

Don't wait until your senior year.

I also feel strongly that you should not hold off on studying abroad until your senior year. Although you're nowhere close to being a senior yet, think about it: the last thing a senior college student needs is to come back from study abroad and have trouble transferring credits and then not be able to graduate on time. When I returned from study abroad, I was surprised when the office told me that it could take up to six months for the grades to come and credits to be transferred. Now, if you're on the five- or six-year plan, this probably doesn't apply to you so much. But for those of you who need to be out in four, I highly recommend that you avoid a senior semester abroad.

Not only can studying abroad put a cramp in your goal to graduate in four years, but your senior year in college is the last opportunity that you get to party and enjoy your best college friends. Most likely, you will all end up with jobs in different cities and states, so it only makes sense to spend your final year with them (especially when senior year gives you a little more time to kick off your shoes, relax, and have fun!). So stick it out and try staying put your senior year. You can always do your graduate degree abroad.

U Chic Tip!

Before going, I highly recommend meeting with your academic advisor and mapping out what credits you still need in order to graduate. Tell the advisor that you are thinking of studying abroad, and see if they think it is possible for you to graduate on time. Then take that list of necessary classes and look at the possibilities offered to you by study-abroad programs. If you are extremely concerned, make an appointment with the study-abroad office and discuss whether or not studying abroad would stunt your academic progress.

Going after graduation

Don't forget that it is always possible to study abroad after graduation. Even better, there is also the opportunity to complete an internship while abroad that would provide you almost the same life-changing experiences as a study-abroad program. I met people abroad from the U.S. who found internships after graduation. One girl was a design intern for an architect in Florence (an incredible opportunity in a city known for its beautiful architecture) and another one was an intern for a company in Florence that organizes events and trips that are affordable for study-abroad students. Each seemed extremely happy with their decision to work abroad.

You can also go abroad for graduate school. This may be surprising, but there are some well-known foreign graduate schools that can provide equal or better training in your area of expertise. Schools like Sciences Po in Paris or the London School of Economics are top-notch training grounds for budding policy experts or politicians. If not completing your graduate degree abroad, you could get into a program at your college that will send you abroad for several weeks at a time. For example, the journalism school at UNC–Chapel Hill offers several trips to other countries for photojournalism graduate students. Your study-abroad office or website would have more information about the specific opportunities at your school, so be sure to look into these. And don't forget that you should also consider programs offered by other schools. I knew a girl from UNC that studied abroad in Italy through a program at NYU. The great thing about these programs is that they enhance your educational experience while offering something that is perfect for your résumé and for landing that dream job.

AM I SOCIALLY READY?

Besides academics, the decision to go abroad should also be based on when you're *socially* ready for the experience. For most people, studying abroad is a step way outside their comfort zone. Even the independence in college doesn't match the freedom of studying abroad. With this freedom also comes an element of responsibility that you've never had to face before: you are far away from your family and friends.

Some people long for that kind of independence, and the fresh new start that a semester or year abroad offers. But it is also important to understand exactly *what* you are leaving behind. To start, there are many aspects to a person's social life that you have to be OK with leaving behind for a bit: your family, friends, organizations or volunteer activities, and even relationships. Is there a boyfriend? Is a close family member sick? Are you a possible contender for a significant leadership position on campus? Bottom line: don't forget to consider your social life when trying to decide whether to go abroad, or you may end up spending your entire time abroad worrying about what is happening at home. And that would be a waste.

It is important to communicate with the significant people in your life before heading abroad, so everyone knows what the expectations will be. If you find that your boyfriend is not excited to be attached to a girl thousands of miles away, maybe it's time to take a break. But if the relationship means more to you, maybe you shouldn't hop on that plane (but I really do not encourage putting your boyfriend's wishes ahead of your life-changing plans!). Also, you need to be prepared for the reality that you will probably not be able to talk every day by phone. If this is a major sticking factor, try setting up a Skype account if you are going abroad. It is a program that you can download and talk to people over the Internet for free, like a phone or voice chat on AIM. The good thing about it is that if you get a web camera you can see each other as well.

Get your social life in order before heading out

To ensure that your study-abroad experience comes off without any social hitches, set aside time to keep up with friends at home, even if it means sending out mass emails to everyone. You'll be making a new life for yourself while abroad, and with it comes new challenges and stresses, but also incredible benefits. New friends, different roommates, and new dramas will appear. Prepare yourself for all of these experiences, and you will be certain not to run into any social difficulties during your adventure abroad.

AM I READY FINANCIALLY?

Last, but not least, your financial situation will also influence your decision of when to go abroad. This bit of advice should not surprise you: save up money before going abroad. Depending on the current currency exchange rate, it is entirely possible that everything you buy there will be more expensive than at home. Not a great thing. So if your dream is to be in the United Kingdom or somewhere in Europe, be prepared for a credit crunch. If having enough money is a concern, maybe choose to go somewhere with a better exchange rate. But don't forget that currency rates change often, so make sure that you look it up when figuring out your budget before heading abroad.

Save some cash

Saving up money before you head abroad will ensure you have a better experience. Wherever you end up going, you will have many opportunities to travel to other countries and cities that you may never have an opportunity to visit again. The summer before I studied abroad, I saved up a little over $1,000 for travel and souvenirs, and it's no surprise that I spent it all. Most of it went to my gypsy travels to other locales. In the end, I ended up traveling to six different countries! My favorite places that I visited were Dublin, Ireland; Barcelona, Spain; Nice, France; and Geneva, Switzerland. Having some money initially set aside for this extra travel guaranteed that I'd be able to see many places during my semester abroad.

Go for a few scholarships or even grants

Your study-abroad office should have a list of possible grants and scholarships for your study-abroad programs. Some scholarships are specific to programs or countries and other ones depend on whether or not you are eligible for financial aid. If you receive financial aid at school, you should be able to get help with study abroad as well. Your office can provide you with the proper forms to fill out for financial aid, but you need to be proactive in tracking down scholarships to fund your travels. With a little effort can come a big payoff. So don't forget to check out all options.

Working abroad

And don't forget that it is also possible to work abroad. One website, www.workingabroad.org, provides a long list of international internships and work opportunities that are available in many foreign countries. But don't forget to consider the legal restrictions that your host country might have in place. Most likely, the visa that you will receive to study abroad limits the hours you are allowed to something like 20 hours per week. But that amount a week could still provide you with enough spending money to really enjoy your experience. I knew someone abroad who scarcely spoke Italian when she got there, and she walked into a restaurant only knowing the word for work and the owner gave her a job. Moral of this story: if you want a job, even if there are language differences, it is very possible that you can land yourself with a sweet and, who knows, fulfilling job experience that you'll never forget.

Study abroad is a life-changing experience no matter how many times you've heard it. Step outside of the box and take a chance. Just make sure that you're fully prepared before you take the first step.

U Chic Essentials—The College Perks

Use your summers wisely

We cannot emphasize the importance of this tip enough. Don't just go home and get whatever job comes your way. Be on the lookout, during your freshman year, especially early on in the second semester, for a summer internship opportunity in your field of interest.

Network often

Getting serious about your future? Start going to as many networking events as you can. These events are definitely worth your time. It's a great opportunity to speak one-on-one with recruiters, giving them a chance to get to know you and even end up being an advocate on your behalf. Why not look even more professional by having a business card handy? You can make one for next to nothing on the Web.

Don't forget about informational interviews

Most people aren't aware of this, but companies—even those that are not currently hiring—are willing to offer you an informational interview. It allows you to gain insight into an industry without having to commit just yet. And you're getting your name out there so when an internship or job comes open there, you'll have someone to contact.

Looking for more great advice? Head to www.UniversityChic.com and look for "U Chic Picks!" for our fav resources and websites—they come highly recommended from our guide's contributors and editors. Be sure to leave your suggestions as well!

CHAPTER 12

What's Next?

Senior year is nearing, and you're starting to wonder, "What's next?" Great question. Maybe you're considering grad school. Or is heading to the real world the best next step? And some of you may have no clue. No worries—although we can't promise to help you figure it all out, we definitely have some great advice. So sit back, relax, and enjoy our last chapter and your time in college because the future is looking great no matter what you decide next!

the case against grad school

Maura Judkis, The George Washington University

I've got bills to pay. A year out of school, I've realized that bills are what separate the grown-ups from the not-quite-there-yets. The sooner you have to pay them, the quicker you grow up. That's one of the reasons that I went straight into the workforce after graduating from The George Washington University, rather than piling on more student loans for another degree.

As a journalism student living in Washington DC, I helped pay my way through school by working for several publications while taking classes (and being extremely thrifty!), so I already felt very much a part of the working world by the time I graduated. A master's in journalism wasn't something I really needed to get a job, and after 16 years of education—well, I was tired. Tired of papers and research and required reading, when all I wanted to do was just get out there, write, and learn on my own terms. Some people say that going straight from undergrad to grad school will help you keep up a student momentum, but let's face it: most seniors, confronted with the prospect of quickly dwindling college days, are making the most of their friendships, not their final moments in the classroom. Senioritis beats momentum any day.

At the same time, the job search can be tough in competitive fields, which makes the idea of grad school very appealing. I spent 3 difficult months interviewing for every journalism job I could find, shuttling myself between friends' couches in Washington DC and New York and my parents' house in Pittsburgh, freelancing all the while. I am glad that I held out through those tough decisions, though—the job I ended up getting was a perfect fit for me.

Working is a welcome break from the classroom environment. It feels fantastic to come home from work and have my evenings to myself, rather than worrying about studying for a test or writing a paper. I feel challenged by my job, but without the pressure-cooker environment of exams and grades, my stress level has halved. I read books on my own timeline. The only thing I've envied my straight-to-grad-school friends for is the enhanced opportunities they have to meet new people, which can be harder when you've left the melting-pot environment of college. That and the leisurely winter, spring, and summer breaks, of course.

I'm not sure when I'll go back to school, or even what I'll go back for. I do know, however, that the continuance of my education will depend on that defining keystone of my grown-up criteria—bills. I hope to finish paying for my first degree soon, and then I'll be looking for someone else—an employer or a scholarship fund—to pay for the next one. It could be in two years or ten. I'll know when I'm ready. Until then, I'm reminded of a favorite quote from one of the chicest ladies, Dorothy Parker, on my chosen career: "I'd like to have money. And I'd like to be a good writer. These two can come together, and I hope they will, but if that's too adorable, I'd rather have money." College, straight to career—well, it's not too adorable for me.

Should you delay grad school for a job? If you agree with any of these following statements, a few years of work experience might not hurt.

WHAT TO DO WITH MY LIFE?

Every girl struggles with uncertainty in her senior year, but if you truly have no idea what you want to do, it's best to try out different careers before committing to several expensive years of school that you may not even like. I've known older friends to collect degrees like accessories. One girl toiled away at a master's in English, only to graduate and decide that her true passion was to be a personal trainer. Another friend got a degree in library science, and then took paralegal courses—neither of which has been very crucial to his current position as a marketer. And he still doesn't know what he wants to do with his life, but with so much school to pay off, he lives with his parents. A few years testing out library and legal careers would have saved him the costly decision. I know he doesn't feel he wasted the time—no time spent learning is wasted, after all—but he certainly doesn't feel like he has a head start on his peers.

I AM UP TO MY EARS IN DEBT

So why add more? If you can get a full ride to grad school with a stipend, that helps—but they only go out to a select few. Grad school costs a lot of money, and can be way more intense than undergrad. You may find it difficult to hold a job while in school. Best to go to work and pay down your debt for a few years until it's manageable. Your employer may even help defray the cost of grad school with a tuition assistance program.

I DON'T NECESSARILY NEED THE DEGREE

In journalism, the number of degrees you've obtained doesn't entitle you to a higher salary—rather, it's the quality of your writing, and the reputation of the places you've been published. This holds true for several other professions. One friend got a master's in public policy, and later found himself working as a researcher at a nonprofit, where he was the only person with a higher degree on his team. After spending a lot of time and effort on a master's, he was frustrated and doesn't think he'll be there long. Ask other people in your field if they think a master's is crucial to getting your foot in the door, and if they say no, test the waters by applying for a few jobs. After all, you can always go back to school after a year or two.

FRANKLY, I'M REALLY BURNED OUT AFTER UNDERGRAD

One argument for going straight to grad school is that you maintain the habits and pace of student life. However, by the end of senior year, some girls just want to be out the door and done. There's nothing wrong with this—after all, you've spent the last 16 or 17 years of your life in school, and it's natural to want something different. If you're burned out but know that grad school is in your future, take a year off to travel, work, and learn for your own sake. Read all of the books that you were too busy to finish when you were in school. Do some additional research on your thesis, so you'll still be on top of your game when the application season rolls around next year. Figure out who you are outside of school. You'll be a far more well-rounded and polished candidate with a year or two of grown-up work under your belt, compared to the people who are applying straight out of school and know nothing outside of academia. Also, the mental break will refresh your brain and improve your attention span for school—and get you right back into your pre-senioritis momentum.

why I chose grad school

Monica Taylor, California State University – Los Angeles

hould I go to graduate school? What is the best program for me? I'm not sure I want to go. What if I never go back to school? What if I get a graduate degree and then change my mind? Can I afford it? I'm tired of school; maybe I'll wait—is that OK? These questions plagued me incessantly in the months before college graduation. And I know I was not alone. Experts say that graduating from undergrad is one of the hardest times in one's life. It involves massive transition in almost all areas of existence: work, school, living situation, and the list goes on.

If you already know that you need an MA or a PhD to get your dream job, and you are certain that's what you want to do, then go for it! Do whatever it takes to get there. But if you're like me and think you should go to grad school but still have many unsettled questions, take your time, do your research, talk to your mentors and advisors, and then decide. You should not feel rushed or stressed at any point. The best decisions in life are usually made on your own terms. Here's how I made mine.

I went to California State–Los Angeles for my undergrad. I got a BA in history and a minor in women's and gender studies. I am in love with history, and if I could marry school, I would. I love class. I love reading. I love learning more than almost anything. Now, don't stop reading because I'm a nerdy bookworm and you're not. I'm just trying to set up the background. My plan was to be a professor—Dr. Monica Taylor, professor of U.S. women's and social history. At some point I began to wonder if that was what I really wanted. What if I went to the trouble to get an MA and then a PhD, and then changed my mind?

> My plan was to be a professor–Dr. Monica Taylor, professor of U.S. women's and social history. At some point I began to wonder if that was what I really wanted. What if I went to the trouble to get an MA and then a PhD, and then changed my mind?

I was also scared that if I took some years off from school to decide, I would never go back. Both were very scary options.

So, with all this stress, how did I move forward? First, I decided that it was OK for me not to know or have a plan. I used to dread people asking me what I wanted to be in the future because I hated saying, "I don't know," or, "Maybe a professor, most likely." Once I got past worrying so much what other people thought, I felt more at ease to make the decision that was right for me. So be OK with where you're at; you don't have to conform to anyone's standards or feel embarrassed for not being sure.

After I quit caring what others thought, I took an inventory of myself. It may surprise you, but this doesn't take as long as you would think. I sat down and made a list of what I'm good at. What are my skills and my natural talents? For me, they are academia, reading, teaching, and helping people. Next, I thought about what my passions were. After writing down social justice, education, history, and women's issues, I realized that my list of talents and passions made a pretty strong argument for going forward in my dream of being a professor. And I did. Currently, I am a graduate student at Cal State–LA, working on my MA in history.

Now, I am still not completely sold on being a professor. But taking the time to figure out my real passions has put me in a place where I know that whatever I do—whether becoming a professor or something else—will require maybe not a PhD but definitely a graduate degree. You can do the same thing. What are you good at? What are you passionate about? What direction does that pull you in? Start with these questions, and you are putting yourself one step closer to making the right decision.

I hate to break it to you: it's going to be a little scary no matter what you decide, grad school or not. There is always that little concern that you're not making the right decision, but that's life.

We can't predict the future, but we can make an informed decision. And remember, you're not alone; every graduating college student faces these challenging questions. But relax a little, take time to think and talk about it. You don't have to have everything perfectly planned out; the goal is to just figure out what is best for you.

say bye-bye to grad anxiety

Katie Reynolds, Central Connecticut State University

*D*oes the thought of graduation bring a rapid heartbeat or even sweaty palms? Or maybe it makes you a little nauseous? You might be suffering from a case of grad anxiety. Guess what? It's completely normal. Trying to cope with the stress of graduation is no piece of cake, but there are ways to take it in stride. Sure, leaving friends who have become your life for four years is hard enough, let alone trying to find a job or a new place to live or even adjusting to a move back home with your parents again. All of this can be super-stressful. It's important to remember that you're not in this alone. In fact, there are millions of college seniors across the U.S. facing the same pangs of anxiety that you're feeling at this very moment. The trick is to not allow the stress to take over and make you feel hopeless. This section is all about how you can relax and enjoy your final year even when the future is still a question mark.

RELAX A LITTLE!

First, take a deep breath.

In between preparing for the big move, a new job, or even simply the unknown, take time to *relax*. Whether it be exercise, television, writing, or just enjoying times with your friends, take advantage of any time that you have for yourself. The stress has been coming on fast and hard recently; I've taken all of the nervous energy and channeled it into exercise. Every time I start to feel overwhelmed with all of the work I have to do, I hop on the treadmill and work off those nerves.

Go brunching!

One of my favorite things to do during college was grab brunch with my girlfriends on the weekends at the school cafeteria. We would all roll out of bed, throw on our sweats, and meet at the café for a long, relaxing meal. There were never any time limits, nothing was rushed and we could just sit there and gossip for as long as we wanted. You certainly won't ever get your college days back, so you might as well take advantage of the time you have left.

Pamper yourself

No matter how hectic your schedule may be or how much the stress is building, be sure to give yourself a little TLC once in a while. Consider going for a massage or having a spa day with your friends. It will be a great way to temporarily escape the stress. And who doesn't love a spa day?! If you're like most college students and are low on cash, try something a little less expensive like a manicure or pedicure. And if you really have no cash, try creating a spa day of your own with your friends! I did this a few times with my girls. We'd paint each other's nails, try on new shades of makeup, and occasionally dyed each other's hair. After all of your hard work, be sure to treat yourself to something nice; you deserve it!

ENJOY THE MOMENT

The most important and fun factor in coping with your graduation anxiety is to focus on the *now* and really *enjoy* the end of your time at school. Make the most out of every aspect of college and save the worrying for tomorrow.

Take time to document the memories

I'm a huge fan of photographs. There is no better way to bring back a great memory than to look through old pictures of some of your favorite experiences. I suggest bringing your camera absolutely *everywhere*. I know we're all fans of taking pictures at the bar or at a party, but I mean literally everywhere. Are you having a movie night at a friend's apartment? Bring your camera! You'll find that it's those low-key nights that end up producing the most memorable moments. And then you can have a scrapbooking party at some point with all your friends to create something that will remind you of the fun you had for the rest of your life.

Get out and explore

Take a look around at your campus and the area that you are living and really explore. It wasn't until the end of my senior year of undergrad when I realized how many great activities were being thrown at me, and for free.

Go out!

You're never going to have as much free time as you do in college. Take advantage of your schedule and go out once and a while. I'm not saying party like an animal, but just take time to enjoy yourself. Go out for martinis with your girls, or check out that frat party down the street. Some of my best college memories came from a night out with the girls. There was a bar down the street from CCSU—Elmers. Tuesday nights were "Bar Bingo" nights. We'd all walk down to the bar, play bingo, hang out, etc. It was so simple, but always so much fun.

Take a class for fun

After three years of sitting through several classes that were unrelated to your major, try taking something that really interests you even if it has nothing to do with what you're studying! As an English and Journalism major, I took a *ton* of writing courses but was interested in psychology. During senior year, I took a great psych class the second semester that was really interesting. These amazing educational opportunities are right at your fingertips, so get out there and don't be afraid to try something new.

SO, THE FUTURE IS STILL UNKNOWN. SO WHAT?

Most of you have spent a good portion of your life planning for what comes next. However, when college graduation approaches, sometimes it is not always clear what the best next step will be. Although this realization can be a major stress, it really shouldn't be. After all the hard work that you've put in over the years, you owe yourself a break. Take some time. Travel. Live in a different city. No matter what, it's worth your time because every new experience is an opportunity for growth.

As graduation gets close, it's really important to cherish the friendships that you've built and appreciate everything your school has given you over the last four years. If you've made your best effort to prepare for the future, then there is really no need to worry too much about what's ahead after graduation. Prepare what you can, give yourself some time to relax, and truly enjoy the life that you have built for yourself as a college student. Your anxiety is certain to melt away.

U Chic Essentials—What's Next?

Don't forget your goals

A proven method for making your dreams come true is to self-actualize. What do we mean? Dream it, write it down, and go back to your goals over and over. The more you envision where you want to head, the more likely you're going to make it happen. And if your goals change, that's completely OK. That's the point of having goals in the first place—to always be in tune with what you really want and then not being afraid to change course if necessary.

Slow down a bit

As you near graduation, don't be in such a rush. Take time to relax and really make the most of your time in school. You'll have the rest of your life to work, but you won't be with these people forever. Brunch with your girlfriends. Visit those museums that you've always wanted to see but for some reason never found the time. Now is the time to really build bonds that will last a lifetime.

Go for nontraditional jobs

No one said that you had to put on a suit and go to a 9-to-5 job the next day. Consider living and working abroad for a year or moving to a place like New Orleans to get involved in the community for a year. These nontraditional experiences are great ways to make money (though, maybe not quite as much as your accountant friends) while seeing a part of the world that many others never get to see. And who knows where it might ultimately lead you.

Looking for more great advice? Head to www.UniversityChic.com and look for "U Chic Picks!" for our fav resources and websites—they come highly recommended from our guide's contributors and editors. Be sure to leave your suggestions as well!

acknowledgments

. . . .

*T*his book is the product of a lot of hard work, support, and passion from a group of people that I love dearly. Thanks must first go to my agent, Loretta Barrett, and my Sourcebooks editors, Hillel Black, Erin Nevius, and Sara Kase, for helping me turn the inspiration behind UniversityChic.com into a book. Thanks to the team at UniversityChic.com. Kirthana Ramisetti and Jim Jenkins for keeping the spirit alive. Many thanks, also, to Laurie Bainter, Director of Student Persistence at College Bound in St. Louis, Missouri. Laurie was a tremendous help in connecting with several of the contributors to this guide. I also want to thank my parents, Jim and Nancy, and my grandparents, Bill and Mary Lou, for their endless support. You have always been there for me, reminding me that anything is truly possible in this life. Thanks to my lifelong partner and soul mate, Matt. You're a genius in every sense of the word. I saved my last acknowledgment for Kristy Leong, one passionate and brilliant woman who has supported University Chic from the very beginning. I am so lucky to have met you that day at the University of Pennsylvania. I look forward to more creative endeavors to come.

contributors

· ·

Kara Apel, University of South Carolina

Olga Belogolova, Boston University

Maggie Biunno, Hofstra University

Janine Camara, University of North Carolina–Greensboro

Miryam Chico, Kean University

Nisha Chittal, University of Illinois–Urbana-Champaign

Johannah Cornblatt, Harvard University

Jessica Cruel, University of North Carolina–Chapel Hill

Allison Davis, Barnard College

Donyel L. Griffin, Kean University

Melanie Harris, Virginia Tech

Harmony Haveman, Pacific Lutheran University

Aja Johnson, University of Maryland–College Park

Lativia Jones Bolarinwa, University of North Carolina–Chapel Hill

Maura Judkis, The George Washington University

Emily Kaplan, University of California–Davis

Hannah Kong, Virginia Tech

Kathryn Lewis, University of North Carolina–Chapel Hill

Krista Naposki, Elon University

Pamela O'Leary, University of California–Berkeley

Briana Peppers, Spelman College

Anna Prestek, University of Washington–Seattle

Katie Reynolds, Central Connecticut State University

Alexa Rozell, Georgetown University

Jennifer Rubino, Kean University

Amanda Sandlin, Rider University

Kristyna Serdock, Stony Brook University

Jillian E. Sorgini, Hofstra University

Erica Strauss, Kent State University

Monica Taylor, California State University–Los Angeles

Alyssa Vande Leest, University of Wisconsin

Raneisha Williams, Ripon College

index